WILLY BRANDT

A Biography

by

Alma and Edward Homze

THOMAS NELSON INC.
NASHVILLE / NEW YORK

Copyright © 1974 by Alma and Edward Homze

All rights reserved under International and Pan-American Conventions. Published in Nashville, Tennessee, by Thomas Nelson Inc., and simultaneously in Don Mills, Ontario, by Thomas Nelson & Sons (Canada) Limited. Manufactured in the United States of America.

First edition

Library of Congress Cataloging in Publication Data

Homze, Alma.
  Willy Brandt, a biography.

  Bibliography: p.
  1. Brandt, Willy, 1913–   I. Homze, Edward, joint author.
  DD259.7.B7H6   943.087′092′4 [B]   74-3273
  ISBN 0-8407-6391-3

Acknowledgments

The authors gratefully acknowledge permission to reprint materials from the following sources:

David Binder, "Willy Brandt: A German Life." *The New York Times* (November 30, 1969). © 1969 by The New York Times Company.

Hermann Otto Bolesch and Hans Dieter Leicht, *Willy Brandt,* trans. by Alice Denes (Tübingen, Germany: Horst Erdman Verlag, 1971), pp. 40, 50. © 1971 by Horst Erdman Verlag. Trans. © 1971 by Alice Denes.

Willy Brandt, *In Exile: Essays, Reflections and Letters, 1933–1947* (London: Oswald Wolff, Limited, 1971), pp. 14, 143, 222, 235, 238. © 1971 by Oswald Wolff (Publishers) Limited, London.

Willy Brandt

Chancellor Willy Brandt holding a press conference in Oslo's Grand Hotel after receiving the Nobel Peace Prize in December, 1971.

Courtesy German Information Center

Willy Brandt and Leo Lania, *My Road to Berlin*. Copyright © 1960 by Leo Lania. Reprinted by permission of Doubleday & Company, Inc.

David Childs, *Germany Since 1918* (New York: Harper and Row, 1970), p. 112. © 1970 by David Childs.

Angel Flores (editor), *An Anthology of German Poetry from Holderlin to Rilke* (New York: Doubleday and Co., 1960). "A Streak of Blood" by Stefan George (p. 294). © 1960 by Angel Flores.

Klaus Harpprecht, *Willy Brandt. Portrait and Self-Portrait* (Los Angeles: Nash Publishing Company, 1971), pp. 12, 13, 30, 33, 34, 36, 40, 198, 226, 227, 228, 231. © 1971 by Klaus Harpprecht.

Christoph Meckel, "The Peacock," trans. by Christopher Middleton in *German Writing Today*, edited by Christopher Middleton (London: Penguin Books Ltd., 1967), p. 227. © 1967 by Christopher Middleton.

Also by Alma and Edward Homze
Germany: The Divided Nation

By Edward Homze
Foreign Labor in Nazi Germany

To

Kim, Rex

Susanne, Joan

Contents

I Wild-Eyed Youth *13*
II "Politics Will Ruin Him" *26*
III Exile *36*
IV Years of War *47*
V Return for Reconstruction *59*
VI The Blockade *73*
VII A Career in Politics *77*
VIII Warrior for Berlin *92*
IX The Candidate *111*
X Chancellor of Reforms *122*
XI Moments for Privacy *142*
XII A Man for All Europe *156*
Glossary *166*
Index *168*

CHAPTER I

Wild-Eyed Youth

The facades of the old buildings of Lübeck, often decorated with alternate courses of red brick and glazed black brick, tell of the rich history of that north German town. The windows, old and wavy, reveal interiors containing rough-hewn wooden tables, pew benches with tall backs, copper lamps and lanterns, and ships' models—all the furnishings of seamen's taverns. The wharves of Lübeck shelter the ships descended from the great ocean vessels of the Hanseatic League, the association of towns that monopolized trade with Russia and Scandinavia from the twelfth to the sixteenth centuries.

The canals, which lace the city together, are intersected by streets, some of them too narrow for two people walking abreast and certainly too small for automobiles. The towers of the city now house the local museums of history.

It was here in this ancient business center of northern Europe, a town rich with a heritage of sea life and lore, that Willy Brandt was born. Here he was educated and began his work in Germany's Social Democratic Party. It was here that the man was shaped.

Who was this man who grew up surrounded by the history of an old and proud seaport? He was not known as Willy Brandt then. His name was Herbert Ernst Karl Frahm. He remembers himself as an eight- or nine-year-old boy standing in front of a bakery window and staring longingly at the bread and rolls inside. They looked so crisp and they smelled so good that they made him feel slightly dizzy.

"Are you hungry, son?"

In confusion Herbert turned around and immediately recognized the man who had spoken to him. He was "Herr Attorney General," one of the directors of the Lübeck Draeger-Works, the company for which his grandfather was a truck driver.

But the employees of the company were on strike.

Herbert swallowed with difficulty, then he nodded. The director took him by the hand, led him into the store, bought two loaves of bread, and placed them in his spindly arms. At once Herbert whirled around and ran away as fast as he could. He was afraid the director would reconsider and take the bread away from him.

He arrived at home panting, and breathlessly told his grandfather about the unexpected gift. But his grandfather was furious and told Herbert sharply, "Take the bread back. This minute."

Herbert did not understand. "Back? What do you mean? The Attorney General gave them to me."

"Gave them—! A striker accepts no gifts from his employer. We will not let ourselves be bribed by our enemy. We are not beggars, to whom one throws some alms. We ask for our rights, not for gifts. Take the bread back immediately."

Filled with confusion and shame, Herbert could do nothing but carry out the order. Proudly he marched back to the bakery; haughtily he put the bread on the counter. "Here—we don't want it!" he shouted. The triumph made him forget even his hunger, and it further strengthened the bond between Herbert and his socialist grandfather.

Herbert's first memory of his grandfather goes back to

Wild-Eyed Youth

the time he was four or five years old. One day a man appeared in a muddy soldier's uniform. He propped his rifle against the bedroom wall, placed his steel helmet on top of the wardrobe, and announced that he was on leave from the front. In his wallet he carried a photo of Herbert. In the picture, the little boy stands stiffly on a chair dressed in an Imperial German uniform, with a spiked helmet, and a wooden rifle under his arm.

Herbert's grandfather came home to visit him sometime between 1914 and 1918, in the midst of the bloody world war that ended with the defeat of Germany and the abdication of Kaiser Wilhelm II. The First World War destroyed much of what Germany had been—its young men, its wealth, and its civilization. The once proud nation turned sour in its defeat. Foreigners viewed with suspicion everything that was German, while the Germans turned neurotically inward, rejecting all that was not "German."

However, in some cases, friendships had been strengthened by letters written during the war. In one such wartime letter, Eduard Bernstein, the German Socialist, wrote, "Nowadays one lives from day to day and scarcely dares to think about the future. But sometimes I hope that when peace comes you and I may meet and shake hands, and tell each other that we have never had one thought of each other that was not kind, and then sit down to consider whether we can help in any way to heal the wounds of civilization."

Unfortunately the wounds were not to be healed. The war had isolated Germany from the rest of Europe, and their defeat and humiliation united the people as a nation and gave new meaning to words like *Volk* (people), *Reich* (state), and *Geist* (spirit).

For the poor of Lübeck, like Herbert's grandfather and

his mother, the spirit of old Germany had been a bitter farce. They were outcasts in a state of the titled, the wealthy, and the powerful. Herbert, born on a cold, overcast day, December 18, 1913, of a little nineteen-year-old shopgirl, was even more of an outcast. Herbert's mother had to give her child her own name. His father was neither known to Herbert nor ever mentioned at home. As an adult, Herbert once said, "I do not know my father and have never wanted to know him. In fact I never even wondered what qualities I may have inherited from him."

Home was a small apartment in a newly built block of houses. There were a couple of rooms and a small bathroom. Herbert's room was in the attic. The rent was fifty marks, as much as Grandfather made in a week driving a truck. Although the old man had come up in the world from his young days as a farmhand on a count's estate in western Mecklenburg, the family still knew hunger.

Herbert's mother could care for him only after her working hours, so during his early years he was left all day in the care of a woman who lived near his mother's shop. He was often left to himself for many hours with no playmates, but the loneliness ended when the widowed grandfather, whom Herbert called "Papa," came home from work. His smell of sweat, leather, powder, and oil entranced Herbert, as did the rough cloth of his heavy coat and his leather belt. Being kissed by a bristly bearded man tickled, and the stories he told of war and poverty and new worlds fascinated Herbert.

Papa told the boy indignantly how his own father had been whipped—placed over a trestle, hands and feet bound, and callously beaten. Corporal punishment was given for even the slightest offense in those days. With that picture always before him, Herbert's grandfather grew into a rebel. He had come to Lübeck to live with his daughter, to work as a factory truck driver, and to become an active Socialist and member of the Social Democratic Party (SPD).

The SPD, founded in 1863, promoted the radical and democratic aims of the industrial working class, but evolutionary, not revolutionary, socialism was the chief characteristic of the party. By the time Herbert's grandfather became a member, the Social Democratic Party was the largest and most important political party in the country.

There were, however, some disturbing characteristics about the SPD that bothered many of the leaders and young members. The party was identified as a "class not mass" party. It was unable to break away from its traditional "workers" orientation, and the broad middle class of voters still refused to vote for it. The party leadership was also becoming conservative and growing more protective of its holdings.

Unlike American or English political parties, the German SPD was more to its members than just a political party—it was a way of life. The party owned newspapers, cooperatives, banks, and apartment buildings; it conducted youth clubs, old-age clubs, and social activities as well as its usual political functions. Herbert's grandfather took an active part in all these affairs. Even his daily work routines were affected by his strong belief that the working class had the strength to rule the country.

One of Herbert's favorite stories involved his grandfather's attempts to thwart the ruling class. In those days it was the custom for landlords to distribute brandy to their laborers just before an election to the parliament. On election day, the men would go to the overseer's home. On a table in the living room stood a big soup tureen. The men walked past the overseer, who sat at the table and recorded their names as they placed their ballots one on top of the other in the tureen. In that way, the overseer could determine exactly how each man had voted.

When Grandfather approached the table during one election, he overturned the tureen, perhaps by accident, and the ballots scattered over the floor.

"What have you done, you clumsy oaf!" the overseer shouted, but there was nothing he could do. He could not find out how each man had voted. Grandfather had cleverly beaten the system!

On another occasion, Papa passionately described the future the workers would have once they seized power. He made it sound like an idyllic world. Refusing to tell Herbert fairy tales, Papa told him instead about the glorious lives of Karl Marx, the great historical Socialist, and of August Bebel and Ferdinand Lassalle, leaders of the new Social Democratic Party. Herbert recalled, "Grandfather also told me that someday there would no longer be any need for money to exist. Everyone would get as much as he was entitled to and at a later stage as much as he needed."

Herbert was drawn by Papa's tales about the war and about a future without wars, about the misery in the country, and about how the Social Democrats would end all misery forever. "No God, no King or Emperor will save us—we've got to save ourselves!" Papa sang to the child on his knee.

To Grandfather socialism was not a political program; it was a religion. To make all men brothers, to eliminate all injustice from the world, even to eliminate money were its creeds. Herbert never tired of listening to these prophecies, and he was stirred when Papa sang the revolutionary song of the workers, the "Marseillaise," "March of the Socialists."

Wild-Eyed Youth

These hours together continued even after Grandfather remarried. Herbert never grew fond of his stepgrandmother, but he went on living with his Papa, and his mother visited him once or twice a week after work.

Around this time Herbert heard for the first time the name of a man who was allegedly his father; it sounded like a Scandinavian name, but the boy was not interested, —or was he? Brandt later wrote, "I don't know. . . . An opaque veil hangs over those years, grey as the fog over the port of Lübeck. Figures and faces are like shadows— they rise to the surface and disappear again, like flotsam on the waves of the northern sea. It is hard for me to believe that the boy Herbert Frahm was—I, myself."

Those were hectic years after World War I, with the Social Democrats holding quasi power. Friedrich Ebert, their leader, was president of the Republic, but their enemies were many and growing stronger. Papa and his friends spoke softly behind closed doors about the danger of German society stepping backward instead of forward. The period was fraught with change. The victorious Allies worked out differences among themselves in a series of compromises, and then invited the Germans to send a delegation to Versailles to receive the conditions of peace.

The Treaty of Versailles stipulated that Poland be re-created, and forced Germany to give up territories that had been annexed in the eighteenth century. Part of Schleswig, a northern province, was returned to Denmark. Alsace-Lorraine was returned to France. These losses, later used by Hitler to instill a spirit of revenge, were costly to Germany both financially and spiritually. The Germans needed a new image, a fresh start, and they looked to the city of Weimar, where Goethe and Schiller had once lived.

There, a new Constitution was drawn up under the direction of Hugo Preuss, himself a symbol of the revolution. As a Jew and left-wing democrat, he had been denied a university career in spite of his merits. Now he, an outsider, drew up the new Weimar Republic, an ill-fated attempt at parliamentary democracy, which lasted from 1919 to 1933.

The first four years of the Republic were a series of almost uninterrupted crises. Bloody civil wars, the reemergence of the military as a strong force in politics, attempts at internal subversion, French occupation of the Ruhr, and frequent political assassinations left the country in turmoil. Indeed, the murder of political figures and the uneven justice meted out to the guilty shocked the people. From 1918 to 1922 there were 354 murders by right-wing conservatives and 22 by left-wing elements. Of the 354, only one was severely punished, although not by a death sentence. Of the 22 from the left, 17 were rigorously punished, 10 of them with the death penalty. Lawlessness pervaded the country.

In February, 1919, the journalist Simon Guttmann spoke for the enemies of the young Weimar Republic. "At the moment, we, the intellectuals, almost without exception oppose the government. The Republic avoids responsibility, does nothing, and is active only in shooting down fellow citizens. Nothing has been changed by the revolution," he said, referring to 1918 as the "so-called revolution."

In 1920 a reactionary coup by the Berlin military was crushed by a general strike of the workers. In 1921 the communists staged an unsuccessful coup. In 1922, after the Foreign Minister of the Republic, Walter Rathenau, was assassinated, the anger of the workers was expressed in mass demonstrations.

In the Weimar Republic, the fantastic inflation that had been plaguing Germany since the war reached its climax in 1923. Herbert's mother and grandfather, like all Germans, had to spend their money as soon as they were paid, because by the next day the money was already worthless. When the new mark was introduced, Herbert and his classmates were asked to collect the old paper money and carry it to school. Big laundry baskets, pillowcases, and tied-up shirts were stuffed with the worthless bills. For each ten billion marks the student collected he got a candy stick, which cost a pfennig in the new currency.

Gradually, between 1924 and 1929, a temporary financial stability returned to Germany, accompanied by a relaxation of political violence and a cultural revival that was second only to the golden age of German literature. Many artists and writers, including Bertolt Brecht, the playwright, moved from Munich to Berlin, a city of growing power in the mid-1920's. Berlin housed government offices and party headquarters, and rivaled Paris as the center of European culture. The composer, the journalist, the actor—all aspired to go to Berlin. One hundred twenty newspapers, forty theaters, and superb orchestras drew the ambitious, the talented, and the energetic like a magnet.

As life settled down, at least temporarily, for the country, Herbert's own life changed. In 1926, when he was thirteen, his mother married. His stepfather was a tall, sturdy, warmhearted builder's foreman from Mecklenburg. The couple later had a son, but Herbert was never close to his brother, for he continued to live in his grandfather's home.

Soon after the marriage, Herbert was admitted to *Real-*

schule (high school), where, in recognition of his standing at the top of his class, he was granted a scholarship. The next year he changed to the Johanneum, Lübeck's prestigious university-preparatory high school, also on a scholarship. An avid reader, Herbert's favorite subjects during those years at the Johanneum were German, history, and religion. He later wrote, "I did not share the enthusiasm of some of my schoolmates for poetry. I was not carried away by the rhythm and the melody of the poems which we had to learn by heart. I was interested in novels which had something to say, in biographies, and first of all in reports on social conditions which gave you a better insight into political problems. Andersen Nexo, the Danish novelist, Erich Maria Remarque, Thomas Mann were my favorite authors."

Herbert was fourteen when he began writing for the local Social Democratic paper, the *Volksbote (People's Messenger)*. The publisher of the *Volksbote,* Jacob Gottgetreu, smiled when he later recalled Herbert bringing manuscripts to the editorial office. "He was promising journalistic material and our chief editor and SPD deputy, Dr. Julius Leber, thought a great deal of him."

Herbert was even awarded a prize for his newspaper writing—a leather-bound edition of James Fenimore Cooper's Leatherstocking tales. With this encouragement, he tried short features and essays. Although the pay was low, five marks per contribution, it was the first money Frahm had ever earned, and it encouraged him to search out new events and incidents that were worthy of description.

During his first years at the Johanneum Herbert was among the best students, but later he began to neglect his studies and play truant. Made to feel like an outcast, he withdrew from the group, became reserved, defiant,

Wild-Eyed Youth

and proud. To provoke his classmates and teachers, he often attended classes wearing the Young Socialist's blue shirt and red tie. A lanky youngster wearing knickers, coarse knee socks, and a dark-blue sailor's cap, Herbert said of himself in those days, "I was a wild-eyed youth."

Herbert later recalled, "The four years which I spent at the Johanneum were an important period in my life, not so much for the very good education I received, but because I entered for the first time a world which, though not hostile, was strange to me. There were few boys from the working class. There were also few teachers who were sympathetic to the young Republic."

Klaus Harpprecht, in the book *Willy Brandt, Portrait and Self-Portrait,* asks, "Did he, son of a poor woman, feel rejected during his high school years, even though he was, according to his teachers, one of the more gifted students? Did he wear the blue Socialist Youth shirt to school out of spite? Was it oversensitivity, brought about by social or personal circumstances that caused him to force his bourgeois schoolmates into discussions that didn't interest them, because they preferred to withdraw into the security of their bourgeois homes—homes whose foundations were already undermined long before they were completely destroyed during the wartime bombings? One might ask him whether, at sixteen or seventeen, he had a presentiment concerning the crumbling—the destruction—of his country. Wouldn't it have been a belated satisfaction had he accepted the offer to become mayor of his home town after his return?"

Political life was important to Herbert during his teens. Under his grandfather's direction, he joined the children's group of the Workers' Sport Association. From there, he advanced to the Social Democratic *Kinderfreunde* (Children's Friends) and the Workers' Mandolin Club. Then he joined the Red Falcons, a group similar to our Boy Scouts, and gradually rose to membership in the Lübeck branch of the Socialist Youth Union.

In Herbert's eyes the youth movement was romantic, and for that reason it appealed to him. Extended hiking to the North Sea and the Baltic Sea and summer camping on an island near Andernach on the Rhine at a Falcons' camp drew him to nature. "I fell in love with the charming hills, with the old castles and ruins, with the mystic legends attached to them. We did a lot of reading and sat up long into the night, discussing the meaning of life and solving the riddle of the universe. Still more important was the practical democracy we learned from our living together. We had to face tasks which we could master only through our cooperative effort. We began to understand the importance of organization and of voluntary discipline. We realized how many—seemingly unimportant—details had to be considered in order to make people of different backgrounds and opposite temperaments work together in the interest of a common cause. And we learned to help ourselves. In our youth movement we had to rely on our own ability and means; we did not expect to be helped or supported by the state."

All the youth movements, not only those to which Herbert belonged, made Rainer Maria Rilke one of their favorite poets. They recited him by the campfire and printed him in their magazines. One of the greatest poetic geniuses in German literature, he left a mark on the lyrics of contemporary writing.

Herbert's experiences in the youth movement were good training for him. His gifts for organizing and speaking became more and more evident on his camping trips. The Socialist Party youth organization in the Lübeck region selected him as temporary chairman, then as local chairman and finally as district deputy chairman. That was in 1929, when Herbert was only sixteen years old. Years later, he said, "As a working-class boy it was easy for me to join the SPD. One might say I was born into it."

CHAPTER II

"Politics Will Ruin Him"

Between 1929 and 1933 Germany experienced years of disastrously high unemployment, government by tightly controlled decrees, a breakdown of middle-class parties, and a resumption of violence. During this period culture became a mirror of events rather than a critic of life. Newspapers and films mass-produced propaganda upholding the radical right-wing Nazis. The best architects, novelists, and playwrights were subdued or silent. The country was overcome with artistic trash, much of which was politically inspired. At the same time, some of Germany's largest business trusts and banks went bankrupt. Germany was on the verge of economic collapse. Everywhere people were turning to political leaders and parties for guidance.

Herbert was finding inspiration and challenge in his activities in the SPD, but in a conference with his mother, the headmaster at the Johanneum warned: "Keep your son away from politics, the boy is gifted—what a pity, politics will ruin him."

But it was too late. Politics were not taught in German schools, but they were his favorite subject. Because of it his fellow students nicknamed him Frahm the Politician. Everyday he found some way to reaffirm his Socialist convictions. Once his German teacher selected him, as the most outstanding boy in his class, to recite a poem at the *Reichsgründungsfeier,* a patriotic celebration of the founding of the Second German Empire. Herbert was unimpressed with the honor. "In protest I put on a bright red tie, with the result that I was sent home. It was intended as a punishment but I was delighted."

Meanwhile, in 1930, his party, the Social Democrats, had split from the government. In that same year the young party members recognized the growing danger in Nazism. "We met the Hitler youth in our meetings and in private sessions, we clashed with them, we fought them with words and fists," wrote Herbert Frahm.

Older party members said that these incidents were not to be taken seriously. The Nazis were certainly not a danger in Lübeck, and they were a small sect nationally.

By September, 1930, however, the Nazi Party had become the second strongest in Germany and, supported by 6.4 million people, had won 107 seats in the Reichstag, the national congress. Their unexpected victories caused even greater schisms in the Social Democratic Party. The Socialist youths ranted against the leadership of the party, and as the number of unemployed rose higher from month to month, they called democracy an empty word. Young people needed work, but the government had none, and the subsidies were "too little to live on and too much to die on."

Even though Lübeck had one of the strongest Social Democratic organizations in all Germany, more and more of the young people and more and more of the unemployed began wearing the swastika emblem in their lapels. Banners, wall writings, and placards openly bore the slogans: "Germany, arise!" "Death to the Jews!" Bands of storm troopers carrying arms beat up and even killed opponents.

The Socialist Youth were not exempt. One evening a scuffle between some of them and the storm troopers left a few young Socialists wounded and a Nazi dead. A trial followed and Frahm was one of the defendants. Since he had not been near the fight, he was acquitted for lack of proof, but his friends in the Johanneum felt that he was disgraced even to be a suspect in a manslaughter case.

In the final examinations at the Johanneum, the students could select one of three themes: history, Goethe, or a statement of a student trying for his high school diploma: "When we look back on our years at school, we must say they gave us nothing for our future life." Only two students in the class chose that theme. One wrote a rebuttal to the statement and thus won the sympathy of the Board of Examiners. The other student was Herbert, who tried to uphold the statement. In spite of his position he passed the examination. His final school certificate recorded outstanding grades including a *"sehr gut,"* or top honors, for religion.

The year was 1932, and Herbert, in spite of his active political affiliations, his publishing experience, and his well-known speeches, was only eighteen.

Herbert had become a full member of the Social Democratic Party before he was seventeen although the official minimum for membership was eighteen. Dr. Julius Leber, editor of the *Volksbote,* leader of the Lübeck Social Democrats, and deputy to the Reichstag, had interceded in Herbert's behalf and was his sponsor. As time passed, however, Leber became more than just a sponsor, teacher, or older friend. Herbert later wrote, "I had grown up without a father; there was an emptiness in my life—Leber filled it. He was a decisive influence in my life."

The relationship between the young, sometimes brash idealist and the older party leader was based on mutual respect. Leber had been born in a small village in upper Alsace in 1891. After he finished the village school as a fine student, a parson recommended him for a scholarship, and he entered high school. He had to give up his studies and return to work, but again someone recognized his talents and he was granted a scholarship at the *Oberrealschule* (senior high school) in Freiburg. By giving lessons to students and writing articles for newspapers, Leber was able to support himself while he attended the universities of Strasbourg and Freiburg. He served in the German Army as an officer, then resigned his commission and earned a doctorate in political science.

Leber came to Lübeck and found the job as editor for the *Volksbote* when he was thirty years old. Herbert wrote of him, "Leber was an 'intellectual,' yet the little people, the workers, regarded him as one of their own. He expressed what they had at heart, he had an unerring instinct for their aspirations and hopes. He had their confidence, for they felt rightly [that] here was a man who knew what he wanted and wanted it passionately. Here was a man who never compromised, not a fanatic, but a real fighter."

Leber obviously lived by his own decree that "personality, strong will, and strong hearts had a heavier weight than the dead apparatus of a political party." Of course the leaders of his own party frowned when he chided them with "stifling the creative energies of the youth." In an article he wrote, "One has tried to prove that there is a conflict between authority and order on the one side, and freedom and justice on the other. We, however, will never forget that freedom and justice, authority and order are dependent on each other; they complement each other. The fullest freedom under a system of anarchy where the state has no authority to intervene practically means slavery for the weak and poor—turning justice into highest injustice." The words could have been written by Frahm himself, so similar in thought were teacher and student.

In the fall of 1931 the Social Democrats were further threatened. The Nazis (German Nationalists), storm troopers, and *Stahlhelm* (steel helmet), a reactionary veterans' organization, united. As a countermeasure the Social Democrats formed the *Eiserne Front* (Iron Front), made up of workers' sports clubs and of the *Reichsbanner,* a democratic veterans' association.

At the same time, the radical left wing of the Social Democrats broke with the party to found the Socialist Workers' Party, or SAP. Herbert Frahm loved the smell of revolt, and he joined the new group, as did a few deputies, many active party locals, and a large part of the Socialist youth. Although small in numbers, the organization was actually stronger than it seemed. There were many disputes about the line of this splinter party, but in Frahm's words, the SAP stood for a strong protest against "ailing, impotent and appeasing" politics.

Leber tried to prevent Frahm from joining the splinter group. "Are you completely mad?" he demanded. "This party is just an association of cripples. Revolutionary? Ha! They are impotents conscious of their physical and intellectual incapabilities escaping into radicalism," fumed Leber, who was ordinarily calm during personal discussions. "In spite of your youth you can appreciate a good book, a fine wine, and a pretty girl. In short, you're perfectly normal and don't belong with those sectarians."

Frahm and Leber fought violently over the issue and parted in bitterness. The split with his mentor and friend left a void in the young idealist's life. He was without his dearest friend. He could no longer write for the *Volksbote,* and his other journalistic income was minimal. In addition, the hope that he might attend the university was crushed, for Leber had promised to finance his studies. Now that too was lost.

In spite of his age, Frahm was made political instructor for the new party and became an organizer and speaker for the Socialist Workers. The work was without pay, so he took a job as clerk for a firm of ship brokers in Lübeck. The job paid him his first regular income, thirty marks a month. He came into close contact with sailors, fishermen, and longshoremen, and he made good friends with his Scandinavian clients. These workers proved to be able teachers, and Frahm took advantage of the opportunity to learn foreign languages from them as well as from books. So his days were devoted to clerking, learning, and fraternizing, while his nights were devoted to politics.

Battles between the Nazis and the Socialists became fiercer. Street fighting and beer-hall battles erupted as weak voices tried to turn the tide of the Nazis. Both the Social Democrats and the Socialist Workers counted on Leber as their spokesman. At a mass meeting he proclaimed: "We are in the midst of a counterrevolution. But we declare: our movement is stronger. History is on the side of freedom, and freedom will be with you as long as you fight for it. Today quite a few may ask what the future will bring. I tell you: the final decision rests with you. It is up to you to decide whether to call off the fight or to go on fighting. I say: we shall fight to the end. Victory or no victory, if one fights for liberty one doesn't ask what tomorrow will bring."

The Socialists all raised their fists in victory and their voices in support of Leber. Frahm was among them. At the peak of the frenzied excitement, Nazi storm troopers stamped into the hall swinging their cudgels wildly. They wanted Leber, who stood alone and unprotected on the platform. Grabbing a chair and smashing it, Leber used a leg to defend himself. He fought free—this time.

Then came January 30, 1933; Hitler was appointed chancellor. The takeover by the Nazis was heralded by torch parades and marches. To Frahm, who was nineteen at the time, two paths lay open. First, he could become one of the "non-Nazis" who conformed to the dictates of the party and restrained their personal opinions, although they did not believe Nazi dogma. Most of the German people followed this course, which was based more on self-preservation than on intellectual choice.

Frahm, however, chose to take the second, dangerous path of active opposition to the Nazis. This choice had its first of many tests only two days after Hitler took power when Julius Leber was arrested. On his way home from a meeting with friends, he was attacked by storm troopers, and although his comrades protected him valiantly, he was severely injured and finally carried off. Although he supposedly had immunity as a member of the Reichstag, he was imprisoned.

Every factory worker, every organization member concerned with Leber's release supported Frahm as leader of a delegation to present demands to the chairman of the local branch of the Free Trade Unions. When the delegation threatened a general workers' strike unless Leber was released, the chairman of the group turned their request down. "I will not read it. Do you not know that according to the last decrees, strikes are strictly forbidden?"

Finally, through the intervention of his wife, Leber was freed on bail for a few days from the prison hospital and

"Politics Will Ruin Him"

allowed to attend one of the most powerful demonstrations in the history of Lübeck. Fifteen thousand people gathered in a field outside town. Although he had agreed he would make no speeches, Leber, his head bandaged, walked slowly up the steps of the platform, paused in the center, and shouted a single word, "Freedom." The shout was taken as more than a demand; it was a vow!

Nevertheless, this was the last free demonstration in Lübeck. It was also the last time Frahm saw Leber.

Later Leber was moved from prison to a concentration camp. He was changed from one camp to another at regular short intervals until 1937, when he was finally released. He then went to Berlin as a coal merchant, a job that gave him a living and also served as a cover for his underground activities. Leber was involved in the attempt on Hitler's life on July 20, 1944, and was sentenced to death by the Nazi People's Court. He was executed on January 5, 1945, and just before he died he wrote, "For a cause so fine and just, one's life is but a fair price to pay."

Frahm's role of active opposition to Hitler's Third Reich took the form of active participation in the SAP which, after the Nazi takeover, was outlawed and went underground. For a while the national party leadership tried to continue its activities, and a secret national conference was called in Dresden on March 12, 1933. Frahm, the young Lübeck party chairman, went there, via Berlin, in disguise to avoid the police. "My less than subtle costume," he remembered, "was a brightly colored cloth student's cap." But even more important, it was then that, after discussing the matter with his closest friends, he called himself by his party name for the first time. Thus, a temporary device for traveling without interference by the Nazis became a permanent identity. Herbert Ernst Karl Frahm, the nineteen-year-old Lübeck Socialist Worker Party chairman, was now known as Willy Brandt.

The train change in Berlin en route to the conference afforded Brandt a chance to explore the city for the first time. He had mixed feelings about the German capital. As a citizen from the provinces he admired its vitality, its great traditional labor movement, and its cultural wealth. On the other hand he distrusted its leaders, its fast pace, its big-city coldness. Lübeck had lovely churches, old Gothic houses, proud mansions—in short, style. Berlin had what? First impressions of the city confirmed Brandt's hesitations. Swastika flags flew from every pole and window ledge. Uniforms were everywhere. Columns of storm troopers marched through the streets. Nazi motorcycle drivers revved up their motors to a roar. Brandt remembers that "the whole city seemed to be an army camp. Only here and now did I fully realize the extent of the catastrophe—much clearer than I had in Lübeck." The Nazis had taken over.

Further disaster awaited Brandt at his conference in Dresden. Some of his friends were missing and had been put in prison or in protective custody. Some, "trying to escape," had been shot. "Incredulously and with mounting exasperation we listened to the first reports about the persecution of the Jews. The humiliations and beatings were nothing in comparison with the horrors of the following years, but already appalling in their malice and senseless brutality. Active opponents of Hitler fell as victims of their resistance like soldiers on the battlefield. But here were human beings, the majority of whom had not even taken part in the political struggle, and they were born as Jews."

As they walked the streets, took the elevated trains,

rode the buses to meetings in saloons or private apartments, the Socialist Worker Party members felt like soldiers on a dangerous mission. "My Germany, my home had become enemy territory. Whom could I still trust?" Brandt wondered. His new friends were Jacob Walcher and August Enderle, former steelworkers, and Paul Froehlich, a writer, all three of whom had been expelled from the Communist Party. They taught the Socialists much about working underground.

While the secret executive committee of the Socialist Party would remain in Berlin, several bases had to be established on foreign soil. From these bases, Socialists could inform the rest of the world about the true situation in Germany. They could also smuggle anti-Nazi pamphlets into Germany and supply spiritual and material aid for victims of the Nazis. One of these foreign bases was to be in Oslo, Norway, where the Norwegian Socialist Party followed the Lübeck Socialists' political theories.

Brandt was given the task of smuggling Paul Froehlich from Lübeck to Oslo, where he was to be head of the Socialist office, but just as Froehlich was about to cross from the island of Fehmarn to Denmark, his unconvincing disguise as a fisherman was uncovered, and he was arrested. Brandt was the alternative for the Oslo base. He could no longer stay in Lübeck, for he would soon be arrested for his anti-Nazi activities. He could not hide in another German town, for he could not conceal his political affiliations. There was only one path open to Willy Brandt, and that was to Oslo.

CHAPTER III

Exile

The first rays of the sun had not yet broken the dawn of March 31, 1933, when Paul Stooss, a Travemünde fisherman, sailed his small trawler equipped with motor sails through the rough Baltic Sea. A young man in a trench coat was crouched behind some boxes and rope where the customs inspector had not found him. Willy Brandt was traveling to freedom—in the direction of Rødbyhavn, a little town on the Danish island of Lolland. He had but a hundred Reichsmarks in his pocket, several clean shirts, and the first volume of Marx's *Das Kapital* in his briefcase.

But the journey had nearly been aborted before it began. The evening before, Brandt left his hiding place in the fisherman's home to accompany him to a bar for a glass of beer. There Brandt unexpectedly met a former comrade who was now a supporter of the Nazis and who obviously and immediately realized what Brandt planned to do.

"Should I turn and run? Should I ignore him? Should I take him into my confidence as a former friend?" These questions ran through Brandt's mind as he faced his comrade. Thinking fast, he walked over to his former friend, greeted him warmly, and talked with him for many long and anxious minutes. Behaving then as if he had nothing to fear, he walked away, wondering as he left, "Will he follow me? . . . Will he betray my plans? . . . Will he call the police?" When Brandt finally climbed on the boat at midnight, he gave a sigh of relief.

Although Brandt's flight was a necessity, it was a sad decision for him, as it was for the scores of eminent men who fled before or during the Nazi assumption to power. But Brandt's name was on the Nazi black list, and he was needed in Norway to set up a series of foreign contact points for the SAP.

Despite the great power of the Socialists in the 1920's, Adolf Hitler's Nazism was able to destroy the SAP in Germany rather easily in 1933. Many of its leaders were arrested, while some, like the young Brandt, escaped abroad, and others went underground to work against the Nazis. Everyone felt that the party would have to be re-formed to serve a new Germany after Hitler's defeat, and Brandt's job in Oslo was to forge a valuable connection between the party foundation and foreign workers who would help rebuild it.

At the same time Brandt had to leave his name, his family, his home, and his party friends behind in Germany. Among them was a girl named Gertrude, to whom he wrote regularly. Brandt included in his letters anti-Nazi slogans written between the lines with invisible ink. Once, when Gertrude was called to Nazi headquarters for interrogation, she suddenly remembered a letter from Brandt in her purse. Quickly she chewed up and swallowed the paper and returned home safely after questioning.

Gertrude left Germany and arrived in Oslo a few months after Brandt. There she helped him put his hotel-room-suitcase existence to order and assisted him with his correspondence.

The *Arbeiterbladet* was the newspaper of the Norwegian Labor Party, and as soon as Brandt arrived in Oslo, he turned to its foreign editor, Finn Moe, for help. Eager to aid a fellow comrade, Moe saw that Brandt was given a small monthly allowance from a special fund set up by the Norwegian trade unions. Since Brandt also volunteered for some party clerical work, he received double pay and a housing allowance, but within several months he gave up this financial aid because his income from writing was enough to support him. His journalistic articles were distributed to several dozen newspapers, and his feature stories were popular with the trade-union magazines.

In his writing, Brandt tried to keep in mind the advice of his mentor, Julius Leber. Once, when Brandt had written something hastily and ill-advisedly, Leber had said, "You know how to write. But why don't you let your articles lie on your desk at least one night before you send them off to press? The next morning, looking at your manuscript, you yourself will probably find that some rewrite might be in order. As a result, your articles will improve, don't you think?"

Because of his writing, Brandt's life was secure though simple. He later said, "When you are young you don't mind dry bread for breakfast and a cheap lunch at the feeding center."

Although Brandt had come to Norway on a political mission, he was determined to be a part of Norwegian life as an activist and not as a spectator, like most émigrés. "Much as I was concerned with the sorrows and troubles of my companions in misfortune, I realized the necessity of taking root again. I did not want to be an outsider. My youth had something to do with this decision. I refused to live in a spiritual and political isolation," he said.

Brandt threw himself into his mission. He managed the Oslo SAP organization and was chairman of the local refugee association. He spent some time with the Norwegian youth movement, worked for the education branch of the

Norwegian Workers' Party, and was secretary of the Norwegian public relief scheme.

Brandt could already read Norwegian when he arrived in Oslo, and he made sure that a few weeks later he was speaking it well enough to be understood. Several months after that he delivered his first public speech in Norwegian, and before long he was speaking that language as easily as his mother tongue.

The more Brandt became involved in the life of the Norwegians, the happier he became. "My work with the Norwegian Youth Federation belongs to the happiest chapters of my life," he reflected. "There I made friends with men and women who later were to assume a high responsibility for the affairs of their country: Rakel Sewerun, who became a deputy and Minister for Social Affairs; Nils Langhelle, in later years Minister for Defense and President of the Parliament; Halvard Lange, the Foreign Minister, well known and much liked far beyond the confines of his country."

The Youth Federation itself was a mass movement. Not only did they talk politics, they also gathered to enjoy dancing and music. Although they knew the literature of Scandinavia well, they were curious about intellectual trends in Western Europe and in America. Brandt's background placed him in the position of "expert on foreign affairs," and he was more and more in demand as a lecturer. In this position he taught others much and also kept himself informed through questions and conversations with members of the audience.

Brandt's lectures about the true nature of Hitler's Germany helped him maintain ties with various groups of German exiles in Denmark, England, Holland, France, and Czechoslovakia. By now, Brandt had to describe the worst. In 1933, with Hitler's assumption of power as chancellor and the birth of the Third Reich, the Nazis began a rule of violence. The regime was soon characterized by genocide, euthanasia, secret police arrests, and concentration camps.

Brandt's concern was how to help the Germans who had stayed behind to fight the Nazis actively. He went to Copenhagen to meet other political refugees and to exchange ideas with them and comfort them. The city was an excellent site for such secret conferences with friends from Lübeck and other parts of northern Germany.

Brandt's group carried on "illegal" correspondence with people in Germany by using invisible ink to write personal or political messages between the lines of letters. The émigrés published "illegal" newspapers and pamphlets and smuggled them across the border in false-bottomed suitcases and empty fake books. Unfortunately only a small percentage of them actually reached their destination.

Brandt's intellectual life during this time received a great stimulus when a friend put him in contact with a special group of Norwegians called Mot Dag ("Toward a New Day"), radical Socialists who led Oslo's social and intellectual life. Students, writers, and scientists belonged to this group, which for many years was the center of academia. "I owe these men much," wrote Brandt, "stimulating hours, literary discoveries, a broadening of my intellectual horizon."

Brandt helped the group publish a workers' dictionary, but he did not stay with them long. He left Mot Dag because the intellectual arrogance of its members became too difficult for him to understand. "I parted from them with the firm belief that in the world of today there is no place for ivory towers to which intellectuals can retire to lead a life of splendid isolation. On the other hand, my encounter with [the group] . . . strengthened my determination to improve my education. I recognized the need for acquiring a more solid knowledge for my political activity than the one you could gain from pamphlets and party leaflets."

So Brandt passed an examination in philosophy, entered Oslo University, and signed up for lectures in history. He had moved from political émigré to student.

In the summer of 1935 Willy and his friend Gertrude met their mothers in Copenhagen. Later he wrote of the experience, "Two years had passed since I had left Germany. I could hardly believe that it was not more than two years. I felt much older. My Lübeck childhood was far, far away, no ties bound me to my native town. Certainly, I took an active interest in the fate of my friends, and the news of the suicide of my grandfather had been a great shock to me, bitter and painful. I was also depressed by the knowledge that my mother and my stepfather had to endure annoying interrogations and all sorts of chicaneries on account of me.

"But Mother had not a single word of reproach. I must not worry about her, she simply said, I did what I had to do. . . .

"We had no profound discussions, there was no need to explain to each other our mutual sentiments. We knew how close we were to each other and this knowledge gave me comfort and strength."

The Oslo SAP organization continued to write letters, pamphlets, and newspapers for the people who remained at home, and they collected money, which they sent to the

Socialist Committee in Paris. The funds were used for the support of families of prisoners, for legal defense, for the funeral expenses of victims—in short, for any victim of the Nazis.

But sometimes something greater was possible. A case in point was that of Carl von Ossietzky, editor of the *Weltbühne,* which Brandt read eagerly. Even before 1933 Ossietzky had had continual clashes with the German law because of his exposures about secret rearmament. Finally, in 1936, after spending some years in concentration camps, Ossietzky, who was suffering from an incurable disease, was transferred to a Berlin hospital.

During his imprisonment the "Ossietzky case" had attained international notoriety. Those familiar with his strong antimilitary position and the expression of that position through his press felt he was a logical choice for a Nobel Peace Prize.

The idea had originated in 1934 among some of Ossietzky's friends and was well received in Norway, but it was too late for a nomination that year. In 1935 former German Nobel Prize winners Thomas Mann and Professor Albert Einstein, among others, supported Ossietzky, and in 1936 nearly a thousand international figures nominated him. Partly because of Brandt's campaign, large groups of Norwegian and Swedish government officials had signed a formal petition on his behalf. On November 24, 1936, the long-awaited decision was announced. The five-man committee gave Carl von Ossietzky the Nobel Peace Prize for 1935. Hitler, suffering a heavy moral defeat, was so furious that he issued a special order: henceforth no German citizen would "ever" be permitted to accept a Nobel Prize.

Nevertheless, many creative Germans were working to preserve their cultural life from Nazi domination. Among them were Max Planck, the physicist who formulated the quantum theory and had received the Nobel Prize in 1918; Richard Strauss, composer of symphonic poems and operas such as *Der Rosenkavalier;* Käthe Kollwitz, painter, lithographer, and etcher, whose works are a social protest against war; Ernst Barlach, sculptor and dramatist; Max Reinhardt, theatrical director, producer, and actor; Georg Kolbe, sculptor and designer of public monuments in Berlin, Hamburg, and Leipzig; Ernst Ludwig Kirchner, artist and leader of expressionism; Kurt Tucholsky, humorist and satirist; Dietrich Bonhoeffer, the theologian; and Gerhart Hauptmann, who received the Nobel Prize in 1912, one of the great literary figures of Germany, whose writings are characterized by a compassion for the poor and a sympathy for men in a hostile world. All of these artists and writers worked to keep their creative spirit alive in the midst of overwhelming odds.

Others, however, conformed to the dictates of the Nazis. They painted or sculpted figures that glorified the heroic individual, unfailing dedication to the great leader, or fervent nationalism. These themes were all acceptable in what was referred to as *Blubo* literature, meaning *Blut* (blood, race) and *Boden* (soil). One of the most outspoken of the "German" authors was Hans Friedrich Blunck, who described the heroic traits of the Germanic tribes and their descendants in the book *Our Dynamic Race.*

Some writers felt it was their duty to remain in Germany and to offer the people some guidance from within. The best known and most courageous of this group was Ernst Wiechert, who, in three speeches, *Reden an die deutsche Jugend* ("Addresses to the German Youth," 1934, 1938, 1945), tried to warn the younger generation of the outrages of the regime. These attacks finally led to his imprisonment in Buchenwald concentration camp. Other writers simply joined the exodus. Over two hundred men and women of substantial literary reputation left Germany when Hitler took over. Thomas Mann, Germany's greatest novelist of the time, was the spokesman for the exiled authors. In political essays and broadcast appeals to the German people (1940–1945), he upheld the proud traditions of centuries of German thought and culture. His brother, Heinrich Mann, recorded the viciousness of the Third Reich in his essays, especially one aptly titled *Der Hass* ("Hatred," 1934). He then turned to biographical and historical works in which he described the triumph of humaneness over the evils of tyranny.

In spite of the dangers in Hitler's Germany, Brandt accepted, in the summer of 1936, a most hazardous assignment. He was to take charge of the Organization Metro, to coordinate the underground work of various resistance groups in Berlin. Preparations for the trip were exacting. The necessary "passport for foreigners" papers were prepared by a friend in Oslo who was an expert in manufacturing documents. Although the papers were official-looking enough, they would not pass scrutiny by the border guards, so a fellow student came to Brandt's aid by lending him his own passport. The expert put Brandt's picture on the passport and Brandt memorized the personal data and practiced the signature. For this short period of his life Brandt became Gunnar Gassland, Norwegian student.

On the day after his arrival in Berlin, Brandt was to meet his contact in the Wertheim Department Store. The meeting was difficult, for Berlin was teeming with swastika flags, soldiers, and strangers. This was the time of the 1936 Summer Olympic Games, and Berlin was the host

Exile

city. The contact was hurriedly made and Brandt was identified to the several hundred members of the party in Berlin. Organized in groups of five, they needed coordination and Brandt was to help them.

Brandt was busy every morning in the Prussian State Library. One by one he read the volumes of Nazi literature, even the Hitler bible, *Mein Kampf*, written in 1923 in Landsberg prison. In 1936 Hitler's foreign policy was paralyzing the world and making Germans everywhere feel that any anti-Nazi movement was hopeless. It was difficult to keep any semblance of a resistance movement active when even the Western powers failed to call Hitler's bluff.

Brandt's identity was tested many times in Berlin. He had rented a furnished room from Frau Hamel at 20 Kurfürstendamm. His landlady had only contempt for the Nazis, and she continually tried to draw Brandt into political discussions. His only armor was to pretend to be an uninformed, naïve Norwegian student who admired German science and culture.

Unfortunately Brandt unexpectedly came into contact with a real Norwegian student. When he was in a bank arranging transfer of his student funds, the bank official introduced him to the Norwegian. "My countryman was very happy to make my acquaintance; I was much less pleased. He immediately bombarded me with questions about my Norwegian home town, about the school I had attended; he wanted to find out if we had mutual friends. I was sure that the Norwegian I spoke was above suspicion but afraid in answering the questions I would give myself away." Finally Brandt was able to pull away from the student but not without wondering how many more times his disguise would be put to the test.

"Soon I had adapted myself to the life of an 'illegal'

person; it was a perpetual pretense and disguise, the necessity of always hiding your true feelings, the mistrust that makes you fear in every chance acquaintance an informer and in every former comrade a traitor, and organization of 'contacts' and secret meetings—my head was full of figures and code words, and they pursued me into my sleep."

One day his landlady told him the police wanted to see him. Since any hesitation or sign of fear would only complicate his position, Brandt went to the police station, only to find that it had been a false alarm.

On another occasion Brandt was sitting in a café when he recognized a friend from Lübeck at the next table. A smile of recognition crossed his face, but they dared not greet each other. The man quickly turned his head, while Brandt rose, paid the check, and hurried away. The frequency of these incidents put a steady strain on his nerves. But such strains were not confined to Brandt. All Berlin, even all of Germany, lived under the tension described in "A Streak of Blood" by German poet Stefan George:

> A streak of blood had gashed a silent town.
> A somber cloud swept out of darkness over me,
>
> Between the thunderclaps I heard the steps
> Of thousands, far, then near. An icy clatter . . .
> And joyful, threatening, echoed a three-forked
> Clear metallic clang, and fury, strength,
> And shuddering horror overwhelmed me.
> As a naked blade then touched my head—
> A rapid, pulsing thud proclaimed the marching hosts . . .
> Everywhere more troops, everywhere the same
> Shrill cry of fanfares. . . . Is this the gods'
> Last uproar over this land?

CHAPTER IV

Years of War

The pace changed somewhat for Brandt when, in February, 1937, he was sent to Spain for five months to act as correspondent for Scandinavian newspapers and to keep up political contacts in Barcelona with his SAP associates. They were five months full of contradictory impressions and important experiences, and they played a great part in determining his later political thinking and actions.

When he arrived in Spain, the Spanish Civil War was eight months old, and within a few months the war turned from an internal problem to one of foreign powers against the Spanish people. "We have to help our Spanish comrades," he wrote to Oslo, "but in order to help we must have the courage to criticize."

The war itself began as a putsch by generals supported by lawyers against a government of free election. It was especially the youth of Spain who fought at the barricades and helped stave off the first assaults of the Fascist rebels. It was especially the youth who filled the ranks of the first people's and worker's militia. Brandt wrote, "The first period of the war has been called the 'children's war.' And on the Guadalajara front Ludwig Renn said: 'I love the young because they seek to do great things. Here in Spain most of the combatants are young and that is why there is so much verve in their fight against Fascism, both in the front line and to the rear.'"

Brandt tried to help organize these same young people into a coherent youth league, and he was able to do it actively, because Spanish was the fourth language he had acquired at the Lübeck Johanneum.

Two factions supported diverse points of view in the war. The POUM (Partido Obrero Unificada Marxista,) or United Marxist Labor Party, supported the world revolution as their overriding concern, while the Communists held the view that the demands of this war took precedence. In spite of Brandt's questions about his own position, he regarded it as his duty to intervene on behalf of POUM leaders who were persecuted, dragged to courts, and even murdered by Communists.

But he did try to describe impartially the double character of the war in a pamphlet: "On the one hand it was a struggle for a new social order, on the other hand a national insurrection against the Fascist invaders. The left-wing Socialists had as their main—if not the only goal—the social revolution, the Communists acted exclusively as auxiliaries of Moscow. And Stalin was, no doubt, interested in defeating Franco, but he was not at all willing to let the Spanish people decide for themselves about their own future. What was needed was a government with only one aim in mind: to win the war and to create the necessary conditions for victory through the centralization of the national economy."

Brandt's writings, his intervention on behalf of citizens, his speeches and his work with youth exposed him to criticism from both sides. To the Communists he was an "agent of Franco" and a "Gestapo spy," while the other side called him a "Communist fighter" for the "Red Front."

It was important to Brandt later to acknowledge his part in the war. He supported as best he could the Spanish Loyalists and did so with great sympathy for the Spanish people. He openly stated that the Western powers would have been wiser if they had not let Spain fall to the influence of the Fascists. He felt that "a different outcome of the Spanish Civil War would have certainly weakened the position of Hitler and Mussolini, and maybe prevented World War II."

In any case, Brandt's literary and political work in Spain was followed by humanitarian efforts on behalf of the Spanish people when he returned to Oslo. Medical supplies and food were provided by the Norwegian Spanish Committee, of which Brandt was secretary. As small as Norway was, the country led this international philanthropic endeavor.

The months in Spain were sandwiched between significant events in Brandt's own country. In 1936, just before Brandt went to Spain, the Rhineland had been remilitarized and the Rome-Berlin Axis, that famed liaison between Mussolini and Hitler, formed. Then, after Brandt had returned from Spain, Hitler annexed Austria (in 1938), and the framework was set up for the Nazi occupation of Czechoslovakia.

The takeover of the Nazis was evident everywhere in Europe, but the tourist season of 1938 was business as usual. The summer resorts on the coast of France and in the Alps of Switzerland and Germany enjoyed a booming season, even as the people were quietly watching the Nazis stomp their heavy boots and wave their swastika flags.

Brandt's work took him all over Europe, and his contacts included politicians, statesmen, writers, and international party officials. But each time he returned to Oslo he realized more and more how much life in Norway meant to him. He had grown in two ways. First, he had overcome the former dogmatic narrowness of his left-wing Socialist position and had become a liberal socialist of the Scandinavian type. Second, but equally important, were the human relationships he had established in Norway. "That these friendships outlived all the troubles and the chaotic confusion of the past twenty years, and that our respective political careers did not dim our mutual trust—that I count among the happiest experiences of my whole life."

Later he wrote that during his time "outside" he never ceased to regard himself as a German despite his Norwegian passport and despite the happy life he found in Scandinavia. Although during the twelve years of Nazi dictatorship he was separated from "Greater Germany," he still "felt close to the millions who were driven to their deaths on the front line or who were alone with their fears in the air-raid shelters."

Then, in September, 1939, Nazi Germany invaded Poland and started World War II.

Brandt had set up a small office in which he worked every morning writing articles and letters, preparing lectures, and writing a book on the war aims. It was based on the idea that the democracies would be victorious and discussed the problems which Europe would face after the fall of the dictators.

Not only was Brandt confident about the future of the world, he was also confident about his own future. He had met Carlota, a young Norwegian secretary at the Institute for Comparative Cultural Research connected with the Nobel Foundation, and in 1940 they set up a simple home, although they had to delay their marriage until later in Stockholm.

Why? At noon, April 8, 1940, the newspapers reported that one hundred warships of the German naval force were

Years of War

passing through the North Sea heading north. This news was followed that same evening by confirmed reports of troop transports in the area. That evening at a meeting of German and Austrian refugees in a community center, Brandt announced that no one should be surprised if German planes were to appear over Oslo the next day.

Before retiring for the evening, Brandt reflected, "The first copy of my book, *War Aims of the Great Powers and the New Europe,* is lying on the writing desk of my Oslo office, 12 Storgaten. Will it find many readers? Will it face the reviewers?" The answer to both questions was no, for this was the eve of the German invasion of Norway. In the early hours of the morning Brandt received a sobering and frantic telephone call. "There is no doubt about it. The invasion of Norway has begun. German warships have invaded the Oslo Fjord and troops have landed at different points along the coast."

At the time Brandt's friends did not know that the Norwegian Embassy in London had transmitted a warning about an imminent German landing in northern Norway. These warnings did not reach Oslo.

Brandt later wrote, "On that morning when Hitler's planes flew across the rooftops of Oslo, I felt it my natural duty to serve the just Norwegian cause with all my might. I was not making a stand against Germany, but against a regime which was devastating both Germany and Europe." And Brandt could best serve Norway in a location safe from the Nazis.

A few hours later, leaving Carlota behind in the care of Norwegian relatives and friends, Brandt, along with leading politicians, drove out of Oslo north via Gjøvik to Hamar, and then to the Swedish frontier. Thousands preceded them, including the King and the government. A few ministers remained in Oslo for a few days to save the Norwegian state bank's gold reserve, which was trucked out of the city and smuggled in fishing boats out of Norway to the United States.

From town to town the government officials and the King moved northward; from Oslo to Hamar to Elverum and closer to the Swedish border, to Nybergsund they drove. One by one the towns received heavy air attack, but miraculously the King and the officials were saved.

Brandt later reflected, "And what should I do? Escape to Sweden? But did I have the right to abandon my Norwegian friends? And besides was it so certain that Sweden would not be attacked and occupied also?"

Brandt decided to remain in Norway and drove to Lillehammer, where his friends from the People's Aid had gone. The organization, which was humanitarian in aim and supported by the trade unions, immediately began collecting woolen blankets and bandaging materials for relief aid within Norway. Meanwhile the King had fled to England, and the Norwegian troops valiantly fought until June 9, when Norway was defeated by the Nazis.

Brandt's position was precarious. In his own words, "I was a civilian. In the Norwegian war I had carried no arms. But that could not save me from the vengeance of the Gestapo. In 1938, Hitler had taken away my citizenship. The following year I had applied for my naturalization in Norway. Trygve Lie, then Minister of Justice, had informed me that I could expect my papers in half a year. Then, after May 1, I found myself in a valley north of Andalsnes—an expatriate German and a stateless Norwegian."

The only access to that valley was blocked. Brandt and his friends considered escaping on skis over the mountains, but saw little success in the plan. Instead he followed the advice of his friends. He discarded all his papers and put on a Norwegian uniform. As a prisoner of war, he would be treated like thousands of others, but as a civilian, he could expect the worst from the Nazis once he was identified. His friends' predictions came true; after four weeks in Dovre Prisoner of War Camp, Brandt was released by Hauptmann Nippers with a free pass to his "home city of Oslo."

The train ride to Oslo seemed excruciatingly long. By wearing a trench coat and hiding his military cap in his knapsack he managed to look like a civilian returning home. In fact, Brandt had been warned *not* to go home but to go instead to an apartment in an Oslo suburb. When he rang the bell, Carlota answered the door and swept away the weeks of anguish and waiting.

But their visit was short. Everyone was endangered with Brandt near, so after a few days he went to a summer home on the Oslo Fjord and lived the life of a hermit. Carlota and his friends visited him, but each meeting held a threat of danger. After much deliberation it was decided that Brandt should go to Sweden, continue his journalistic efforts, and work for the Norwegian cause.

"I left Oslo on July 1, at first by car, then train, and finally by foot. After three days I reached a farm near the Swedish border. The farmer was a Norwegian reserve officer, of great help to me in avoiding the German patrols. He put me on the right paths through the countryside and I was able to cross the border undetected. I reported to the first military post I came to on Swedish soil. The police interned me for only a short period until an old friend vouched for me and I was released. And tomorrow I'll be on my way to Stockholm—a free man."

After Brandt arrived at the comfortable refugee camp on his way to Stockholm, he and Ernst Paul, secretary of a local German Socialist party, talked late into the night.

It was there that Brandt learned that the Norwegian government-in-exile had approved his citizenship. He was now a German who had fled to Norway and a Norwegian who had escaped to Sweden. But his escape was not without pain. Sweden had made some concessions to keep out of war and maintained a strict neutral policy in spite of her support and sympathy for Norway. Although this was difficult for Brandt to understand, he used his time well. He spent his days in Stockholm in predominately Norwegian surroundings.

Contact with the Norwegian resistance movement was, however, on a personal rather than on an organizational level. Even close and intimate friends had been shot as hostages or found dead in other ways. He kept close contacts with the Stockholm author Ture Nerman and the editors and sponsors of the magazine *Nordens Frihet*. He spent his days there writing articles about the Norwegian campaign, which later became the basis of a book published in Switzerland in the German language. During this time he also wrote three books that were published after the war. One was a two-volume study of wartime Norway and the other a study of guerrilla warfare.

Brandt did a great deal of writing in Norway. At the same time he was active in the refugee organization and acted as chief editor in his own business, the Swedish-Norwegian Press Agency, through which he furnished news to keep foreign presses informed of the resistance movement against the Nazis.

Although Brandt was productive in Sweden, he was not without concern for his own safety. His years in that neutral country were not as secure as many imagined, because there was always the danger that it too would be invaded. To prepare for every eventuality, Brandt applied for entry into the United States. "Swedish officials have advised me to leave Sweden," he noted. "If Sweden's position were to become more exposed there is no guarantee for my personal safety. I have already been deprived of German citizenship and I have definite news that the Gestapo have tried to trace me in Norway."

In the spring of 1941 Carlota came to Stockholm with their newborn daughter Ninja. Moving into a small house, the Brandts had a normal family life for the first time. Their friends included a young author, Torolf Elster, and Professor Gunnar Myrdal, who later became widely known in the United States through his studies of the Negro problem and his activities in the United Nations.

Even though Brandt counted many influential Swedes and Norwegians among his closest friends, he was not without critics. Trygve Lie, then Foreign Minister of the Norwegian government in London and later Secretary-General of the United Nations, had Brandt in mind when he wrote in his memoirs that he was fed up with the attitude adopted by Norwegians in Sweden. At first they tried to defend Sweden's neutrality and later they explained Finland's participation in Hitler's war in kind terms. "But in my opinion," he continued, "it was going too far when they now seemed to be more concerned about Germany than about Norway's interests and about how to win the war."

Indeed Brandt and his friends were concerned about the rebuilding of Germany after the war. In a pamphlet he wrote with some exiled German Social Democrats, he expressed his concern for his native country: "It should be clear that there exists no underground movement strong and effective enough to assume, alone, power the day after Hitler's defeat. On the other hand, we can hope that the resurgent forces of German labor and democracy will be strong enough to establish and preserve a new order through a coalition of all progressive groups and parties." They concluded that "the democratic re-education of the German people must essentially be the work of the Germans themselves."

Encouraged by Norwegian friends, a study group, the International Circle of Democratic Socialists, met from September, 1942, to May, 1943, and predicted the ultimate defeat of Hitler after the United States entered the war. Members from Sweden, Norway, Denmark, the United States, France, Czechoslovakia, the Sudetenland, Austria, Hungary, Germany, Spain, Palestine, and Iceland participated in study sessions in which they discussed measures to be taken after the war. Brandt, as secretary of the group, resolved that the members of the Socialist movement gathered on May 1, 1943, in the Medborgarhuset in Stockholm should give their support to the work, "Peace Aims of Democratic Socialists!" He resolved, "Wherever freedom was lost, the socialist movement perished also. But the ideas of socialism have lived on and today leave their mark on a substantial part of the discussions on postwar reconstruction."

In 1944, Brandt faced a personal crisis, the breakup of his marriage with Carlota. The pressures of life in exile certainly contributed to the growing wall between the two, and Brandt was plagued by self-doubts about his family life: "Is it all my fault? Should I not have married? Had I the right to bind myself to a woman, to ask a woman to put up with the hazards and uncertainties of my existence? Have I put my personal life in proper perspective?"

Carlota and their daughter Ninja returned to Oslo, and Ninja grew up there. Every summer after the war father and daughter were reunited in Berlin, and Brandt's pride was at its peak when Ninja graduated at the head of her class and became a teacher in Trondheim, Norway.

On May 1, 1945, Brandt delivered a short address to the International Workers Council in Stockholm. As he walked to the platform, he was handed a note. The meeting was about to begin, so he stuffed it into his pocket without reading it and began his speech. Only toward the end of the meeting did Brandt remember the note. He opened it and read aloud the news agency report that Hitler had killed himself.

There was silence. Who could believe that the end would come this way?

A few days later Denmark was liberated, and Sweden began to show the happiness that had been bottled up all over Europe. The celebrations by the Swedes seemed the most frenzied of all, perhaps because of a slight guilt that they had remained neutral while their neighbors, Norway and Denmark, had suffered so much.

Meanwhile there were 380,000 well-equipped German soldiers in Norway and only 40,000 poorly armed Norwegian soldiers. If the German army in Oslo decided to continue the war, a catastrophe would result. Fortunately the German soldiers were given the order to avoid all provocations, and the end of the war came quickly to Norway.

With the war over, Brandt faced the same question as all refugees. Should he stay in his country of asylum or should he return to his own home? Two days after the war he returned to Oslo and then spent the summer months commuting between Oslo and Stockholm. From Stockholm he wrote, "You know I shall always feel bound to Norway by the closest ties. But I have never given up Germany."

In the foreword to his book *After Germany,* he wrote: "I am working toward the elimination of Nazism and its adherents in every country, that both the Norwegian and German nations might live. During these years I twice lost a homeland. I worked to regain two homelands—a free Norway and a democratic Germany. Someday a Europe in which Europeans can live together in harmony will surely become a reality."

For the critics who felt that he had fled his country in its time of greatest need, Brandt wrote: "It ought to be made clear that I did not for one moment regard my fate as an exile as a blot on my copybook, but rather as a chance to serve that 'other Germany' which did not resign itself submissively to enslavement but kept watch for the hour of liberation, and indeed fought and made great sacrifices in the struggle for freedom."

And to his mother he wrote:

> Stockholm
> 26 August 1945
>
> Dear Mother,
>
> I can't yet answer your question about when I am coming. The return of political refugees is now proceeding more rapidly. The American officials, and probably the English as well, are particularly keen to have people back so they can enter the administration and help in the reconstruction of trade unions. So from this point of view I should be able to get a chance of coming back without any trouble. But there are a few things I still have to do here in Norway which I cannot just leave unfinished. But I shall be turning up one day.

CHAPTER V

Return for Reconstruction

The Germany to which Willy Brandt returned in October, 1945, was plagued with postwar problems. Where were the country's frontiers? How should it be occupied by the winning powers? What compensation should Germany pay? What political future did Germany have? What type of state should be constructed? How could a recurrence of Nazism, militarism, or dangerous nationalism be prevented?

The problems of the frontiers were solved by the United States, France, the United Kingdom, and Russia at the Potsdam Conference in August, 1945. The Germans forfeited 24 percent of the entire area of 1937 Germany to the state of Poland. It was further agreed that the remainder of Germany should be divided into three occupation zones, an eastern, a northwestern, and a southwestern. Berlin would be divided in a similar way and be administered by an interallied commandant. The Russians received the eastern zone, an area that completely surrounded Berlin. The United States and the United Kingdom controlled the remaining two zones, and later, France was given a zone carved from the Anglo-American zones. Germany was to be ruled by an Allied Central Council.

Germany had to pay compensation for war damages to the Allied powers, and the nations to receive the greatest compensation were to be those "which have borne the main burden of the war, have suffered the heaviest losses and have organized victory over the enemy." Payment was to come from "the national wealth," such as equipment, machines, ships, and buildings; from "annual deliveries of goods from current productions"; or from the "use of German labor."

What was Germany's political future? The Allies agreed that "it is not the intention of the Allies to destroy or enslave the German people. The Allies want to give the German people the chance to prepare itself to rebuild its life on a democratic and peaceful basis." Implied in the communiqués were a united Germany based on economic unity, equal treatment for all Germans, and the organization of a few central German administrative departments. Although the Allies considered several plans for the division of Germany into states, none became official policy.

How did the Allies intend to "ensure that Germany never again will threaten her neighbors or the peace of the world"?

"By complete disarmament and demilitarization of Germany and elimination or control of all German industry that could be used for military production. To this end all German military, semi-military organizations, even veterans' organizations were completely and finally abolished. All Nazi or militarist propaganda banned, all Nazi-inspired laws abolished, all war criminals brought to justice.

"Further, all Nazi members who have been more than nominal participants in its activities and all other persons hostile to Allied purposes were removed from public and semi-public office and from positions of responsibility in important private undertakings."

In addition to these restrictions, the Allies encouraged the democratization of the judicial, administrative, and governmental systems. Free trade unions and the freedoms of speech, press, and religion were fostered. Among the people themselves, concern for the necessities of life such as homes, food, jobs, and the reunion of families was more important than concern for government or reorganization.

In the newly proclaimed area of Germany, 20 percent of all houses had been destroyed. In certain key cities such as Berlin, Cologne, Hamburg, and Stuttgart, more than 50 percent of the houses were destroyed. In addition to houses for those already there, Germany needed shelter for the millions of Germans pouring in from eastern Europe. By 1948–1949 West Germany alone had a shortage of 5 million dwelling units.

Agricultural output was down; the production of potatoes, rye, wheat, milk, meat, and butter was vital for a country that had 4.3 million more people to feed. In one study of German problems, it was found that only just under 12 percent of the children from six to twelve years of age in Cologne were of normal weight.

Brandt's journey in the autumn of 1945 took him from a scene of energetic rebuilding and excited spirits to a gutted landscape torn by feuds and dissension. About this experience of returning to Germany, he later wrote, "Prostrate Germany was like one of those horrible visions that sometimes overcomes us on the verge between sleep and waking: more real than any reality, and at the same time there rests in a remote nook of the brain the conviction that one is but dreaming, and instantly the ghastly dream will disappear.

"But the surrealistic vision of the destroyed cities, the bombed and burnt-out houses, up and down the streets, the debris-covered fields, the mountains of rubble and rubbish, between which human beings crawled about in the dark like hungry rats, the merciless cold, the unspeakable misery—no, one could not shake off this vision; with every minute it became more urgent, there was nothing beside it, it encompassed heaven and earth."

When he landed in an English plane at the Bremen airport, some of the few friends who had risked maintaining contact with him throughout the war met Brandt and took him to Lübeck to see his mother for the first time in ten years. He had last seen her in Copenhagen in 1935, although his stepfather had visited him in Oslo in 1937. Of course he had lived in Berlin illegally for a short time in 1936, but he had been unable to go to Lübeck, because it would have been dangerous for everyone. Even during the war Brandt could only occasionally risk letting his family know he was alive.

His return was joyous, and his half-brother, who was five when Brandt left for Norway, was now a young man, a veteran of the war, called up in the last months of the struggle.

Brandt heard many depressing tales. Some of his friends spoke of their horrible experience and their own quiet acceptance of their fate. Others talked of bitterness resulting from the occupation. Both sides led Brandt to wonder, "How can so many intelligent, aware, and sensitive human beings, without resisting, quietly acknowledge the horrors taking place around them? How could they have retained any ounce of self-respect while they failed to fight the Nazi regime? And after the war, how could they criticize the powers who freed them from the slave bracelets of the Third Reich?" Brandt admitted that his life had been an easier one, but none of his friends spoke recriminatingly about his decision to fight the war, to broaden his outlook, to strengthen his convictions from Norway rather than within Germany.

Now Brandt was returning to Germany safely, to Nuremberg, as a reporter covering the war crimes trials for the Norwegian Social Democratic Party Press.

The Nuremberg War Trials, from November, 1945, to October, 1946, were designed to punish the former Nazi leaders for three classes of crimes: crimes against humanity, specifically the slaughter of millions of Jews; crimes against peace; and war crimes, such as mistreating or shooting prisoners of war. It was hoped that the trials would clearly indicate guilt for gross misdemeanors, serve as a warning for future generations, and demonstrate that the tribunal of the United Nations could be an effective guardian of international peace. The accused were the surviving major leaders of Nazi Germany. Among them were Hitler's foreign minister, Joachim von Ribbentrop, his chief of high command, Field Marshal Wilhelm Keitel, the head of the slave-labor program, Fritz Sauckel, and Germany's second-in-command, Hermann Goering.

United States High Commissioner for Germany General Lucius D. Clay reported after the trials that of the twenty-four most important Nazis, six were executed, six were given sentences up to life, eight had committed suicide or died, the fate of one was unknown, and three were still at large. During Brandt's assignment he met no one who philosophically supported the defendants. He did meet many who wanted the trials "cut short" and the men hanged without further consideration, and others who wanted the Nazis tried by a German court which could administer its own justice.

"But," Brandt wrote, "even among those hundreds of correspondents who were permitted to attend the sessions there were only a few Germans. As if among all the Nazi crimes the gravest one had not been one against the German people; as if it did not matter how the Germans would accept the evidence presented at Nuremberg."

The Nazis had been guilty of the gravest atrocities and had to stand before international judgment, the international press, and international public opinion. To report this to Norway was Brandt's job.

But the part of his life spent in securing aid for others also found vent during his period in Nuremberg. He tried to reestablish broken ties, to describe the plight of refugees, and to provide for money gifts, parcels, and personal aid for the needy. Brandt wrote, "It is no exaggeration for me to say that a whole younger generation in Berlin owe their very survival of the period of greatest deprivation to the Swedish soup kitchens. A helping hand was reached out to refugees in Germany not only by neutral Sweden, but also by Norway and Denmark, where the wounds of the occupation period were only slowly healing over." Brandt was happy to note that it was Norway which cared for Berlin children in especially large numbers.

While Brandt was reporting the trials and securing aid for the less fortunate, he was also becoming more and more involved with the Social Democrats. The Third Reich had collapsed, but the SPD had an organization and history stretching back many decades. Its record of resistance against Nazism was good, and like other social democratic parties in Europe at the time, its ideas were generally popular.

However, to the party's disadvantage, most of the SPD leaders had spent many years in exile, as Brandt had, and the German public might distrust men who had lived and worked in enemy territory, and charge them with a lack of

Return for Reconstruction

patriotism. Then, too, long years in exile had blunted the Socialists' grasp of the situation in Germany.

Nevertheless, the party was reorganized in October, 1945, with Kurt Schumacher, Erich Ollenhauer, and Otto Grotewohl as its leaders Almost immediately there was trouble. Grotewohl, the leader in the Soviet zone of occupation, suggested a merger of the SPD with the Communist Party. Schumacher and Ollenhauer rejected this idea and worked hard to keep the party independent of Soviet domination.

All the same, in April, 1946, the Soviets forced the merger of the SPD and the Communist Party in their zone into a new organization called the Socialist Unity Party (SED). The SPD in the Western zones refused to do this, thus becoming the first German party to be split by the Cold War.

In May, 1946, Brandt took part in the first party conference, both as a reporter for Scandinavian papers and as a guest delegate for the German Social Democrats living in Sweden and Norway. There he met party leader Kurt Schumacher, a former member of the Reichstag, who had been released by the Nazis from a concentration camp in 1943. Schumacher's great willpower, magnetic personality, and obsession to revive the Social Democratic Party made him, in spite of physical infirmities, the most influential man in the party. However, outsiders saw him as a threat. To the Americans he was "too socialistic," to the English "too aggressive," to the French "too German," and to everybody "too independent."

Schumacher felt that he and those around him were entitled to participate in the decisions of the organization of a free Germany, rather than to have those decisions made wholly by the occupation powers. He felt that eventually the English, French, and Americans would agree—and eventually they did, and some of Schumacher's views were made policy.

In the Russian zone, it was different, however. The Soviets had a clear political concept to put into effect and did so themselves without involving the Germans.

Brandt was greatly impressed with Schumacher and with the various party members around him. Meanwhile he finished another book, *The Criminals and the "Other" Germans*, based on his reports for the Scandinavian newspapers. The book was meant to be two things, a summary of the evidence presented at the trials, and a description of Germany at that time.

Brandt was optimistic about Germany's future, and he had three choices for jobs to follow his work at Nuremberg. First, he was asked to consider putting his name in nomination for the office of mayor of Lübeck. Brandt had begun his political career in Lübeck and had many friends there. Yet he had been away a long time and, with difficulty, he said no. Second, he was offered a leading position with the news agencies in the American and British zones, which were then in a state of transition to civil government. Brandt also refused this position.

A third, quite different offer, was also made to Brandt. Foreign Minister Halvard Lange wanted him as press attaché and political reporter for the Norwegian Embassy in Paris. This position opened the door to a diplomatic career and offered Brandt the opportunity to serve his beloved Norway, but while he was considering the position, Lange changed his mind. The post would not be in Paris, but in Berlin instead. The Norwegian government wanted someone there to keep them informed about political developments in Berlin.

Brandt accepted immediately. His title was to be press attaché to the Military Mission at the Allied Control Council. As such, he would be accorded the semimilitary status of major and wear the insignia "civilian officer" on the left arm of his uniform jacket.

Brandt accepted this post for one year, January 17, 1947, to January 31, 1948. He wrote to friends that he realized it might look a bit peculiar for him to go to Berlin as a "member of the Allied forces," but that he felt the important question was "Where can each of us best serve the rehabilitation of Europe and German democracy?" Since he had supported both German and Scandinavian interests for years, he would continue to do so. "I will act as an intermediary between both sides, in the interest of mutual understanding. . . . It is my first aim to work for peace, for the development and stabilization of European and international co-operation."

In December, 1946, Brandt set off for Berlin carrying a Norwegian passport in his pocket. Berlin, that winter, was a scene of decay and destruction. The prewar population of 4.5 million people had been reduced to 3 million. Half of these had lost their jobs when Berlin ceased to be the capital. More lost their jobs when three quarters of the still undamaged machines and industrial plants were dismantled and sent to the Soviet Union by the Russians. The factories still operating were shut down for lack of coal. The people had no way to make a living. Their houses had been turned into hovels; the buildings were either standing shells or piles of rubble. The winter's cold was one of the most severe in memory. Without wood to burn, people cut up whatever furniture they had left; without warm clothing to wear, they pulled the rags closer; without food to eat, they struggled for a handful of potatoes or a lump of bread.

At the end of the war, Allied officers had considered Berlin completely destroyed—"strategically and politically uninteresting." But underneath the war horrors was the self-respect of the people. The real heroes of the war were the majority of the 3 million Berliners who had somehow survived and now eked out an existence.

Almost at the same time that Brandt arrived in Berlin, another emigrant returned from Turkey: Ernst Reuter. Reuter had once been Berlin's city councillor for transport and had wielded a tremendous influence on the city. Now, after the war, he was to use his statesmanship and his experience in city affairs to save Berlin.

Although Reuter was returning with the hope of being offered the post of lord mayor of Berlin, he was first elected city councillor. The transport department and the gas, water, and electricity works were under his direction. Shortly afterward he was elected lord mayor of Berlin and assumed an even stronger position in the SPD. He felt the Social Democrats should become a popular movement rather than merely a party that defended workers' material interests, and he emphasized that the moral and intellectual hopes of the individual should always be put above the power of the party.

Reuter faced much criticism, especially during the difficult postwar times, when people argued that they could not live on freedom alone. He answered:

"Well, the fish do not live on water either, but *in* it. Man does not live on freedom, but he can only live in freedom. Without freedom people eventually suffocate in a soulless technological machinery, they become ants in a huge mass of ants. The spiritual death will be followed by physical death and by the destruction of everything that makes life worth living." And again, "Since our daily struggle is often and primarily concerned with rather earthly objects, with better living conditions, which we want to make available to everyone, there arises the impression that this is our only aim. But the well-clad, well-fed, well-housed, and well-nursed robot is not what we are striving for. Our aim is the free man, conscious of his dignity and his rights."

Brandt later stated that although there were years between him and Reuter, they were united by common political goals and humanitarian interests.

Brandt was immediately comfortable with the Norwegians in Berlin, but uncomfortable with the broader situation. The Western powers had changed their attitude toward their Soviet ally. This, the beginning of the Cold War, saw Germany at its center and Berlin a pawn for the Russians' strategies and tactics.

During this period immediately following the war everything had to be rebuilt. It was especially important to get the German literary life—literary journals and societies, book publishers, and theaters—moving again. The job was slow, and for the first few years the most effective medium for writers and critics was the radio.

A major aspect of German literature of the period was its preoccupation with moral responsibility and guilt for war atrocities. This theme occurred over and over again in the work of the writers in Group '47, a literary society founded in 1947 by the survivors of Hitlerism. Originally the group was "a loose association of politically engaged publicists with literary ambitions," who felt that the most important functions of imaginative literature were social and political. Among the founders of the group were Heinrich Böll and Günter Grass, the latter described as "a man who can speak to the youth." Grass constantly poked fun at the establishment and became a spokesman for local politics.

Not only did literature suffer from the war, but from 1945 to 1952 Germany had no national anthem. On official occasions a few passages of Beethoven's Ninth Symphony were usually played, but the national hymn sung under Hitler was felt to be so compromised that no one wanted to sing it, even though the anthem was in no way a Nazi song. The words of *"Deutschland, Deutschland über Alles"* are set to a tune from Haydn's "Emperor Quartet." Some attempts to introduce a new anthem were made but never became popular. Finally, on February 2, 1952, President Theodor Heuss restored the former anthem to full status. The action was a symbol that the Germans were once again taking pride in their country.

That Brandt never lost that pride was evident when, at the end of 1947, he became more active in German politics. The decision was precipitated by the suggestion that he take over the Berlin liaison office of the executive committee of the Social Democrats. The position demanded that he deal with the top-ranking Allied officials still in Berlin. But to take the post, Brandt had to give up his Norwegian citizenship and the advantages he enjoyed as a Norwegian diplomat. He wrote to his chief and friend Halvard Lange and explained that an opportunity had presented itself in which he could better serve his own country. The decision to give up Norwegian citizenship did not come easily, but, he continued, "Perhaps I shall experience great failure of my life here in Berlin. But if that should

Return for Reconstruction

come to pass, I would like to meet this defeat with the feeling that I have done my duty."

Brandt's chief released him for his new job to begin January 1, 1948. Lange as well as others lent a voice of support and gratitude that Brandt had chosen to work for the one of his countries that needed his help most.

When Brandt applied for renaturalization in Germany, the document listed both his names, Herbert Frahm and Willy Brandt, but since he had been known as Brandt since he was nineteen, he chose to use Brandt as his official name. The chief of police in Berlin licensed the formal change of name. Brandt later wrote, "As Willy Brandt I had escaped from Hitler's Reich; as Willy Brandt I had worked in exile and returned to Berlin. Therefore I wanted it to be my official name in Germany from now on. The decision was easy since my birth name did not mean a great deal to me. My mother no longer bore that name because she had married."

Some months later, Brandt's papers were official, but if he had waited a little longer before he applied, the application would not have been necessary. According to the Constitution of the Federal Republic, Brandt would have received citizenship automatically. But it was typical of him to apply without waiting. In the biographical introduction to Brandt's book *In Exile,* Terence Prittie writes, "It was probably the sight of Germany's abasement, shame and bitter need which induced him to become a German again. He had no need to do so, he could have had a comfortable, secure and successful career as a Norwegian. Unlike other German émigrés who came home after 1945, Willy Brandt had been completely successful in identifying himself with the country of his adoption and in being accepted by its people. He chose to become a German again in Germany's darkest hour."

In becoming a German again, Brandt chose also to enter fully into the country's political life. The ease with which the Nazis had gained control of the masses had made a particularly bitter and lasting impression on him, especially when he remembered how he and many Socialists of his age had so fervently but unsuccessfully tried to lead the people. In his long years of exile he had had many discussions with his fellow Socialists about the changes that should be made in the Social Democratic Party to make it more effective once Hitlerism was destroyed. Many of its members wondered if the party was not suffering from old age.

During the Weimar Republic, the party had been overorganized, bureaucratic, and suspicious of new ideas and new men. It still was after World War II, even though Brandt and other younger SPD men argued that new methods were needed to solve the problems of the midtwentieth century.

Brandt's speeches and writings after the war were filled with his doubts about where the party was heading. Central to his thinking was concern for the individual and the problem of protecting him from the enormous power of government and modern industry.

Nevertheless, Brandt and the others who wanted reform watched helplessly as their party went down to defeat after defeat in the national elections.

CHAPTER VI

The Blockade

Just before the end of the war, Brandt had met in Stockholm a young Norwegian refugee girl named Rut. That summer they had traveled with friends to see the Sogne and Hardanger fjords, two of the most beautiful spots in all Norway, and they had met many times after that. Shortly after Brandt returned to Germany, Rut followed.

Rut was frightened by the chaotic atmosphere in Germany then, but the hardships of life in a war-torn country were not new to her. Her father had died when she was three. She had been on her own since childhood and had had to earn her own living at fifteen, first in a bakery, then as a seamstress. Along with her sisters Rut had joined the Norwegian Youth Movement at an early age. During the occupation of Norway she had belonged to the underground, was arrested, and had spent some time in prison. Finally she had fled Norway and, after a perilous journey, landed in Sweden. In Stockholm she had worked at the Norwegian Embassy until the war's end, and then found employment with an illustrated weekly in Oslo. Having successfully taken up writing, she was transferred to the military mission in Berlin, where she and Brandt were reunited by their friendship and by their work.

In 1948, despite what Brandt calls "the adverse conditions and our uncertain future," he and Rut were married by a Norwegian parson in Berlin, and they moved into a little house in Hallensee.

The year 1948 was a turning point for Berlin, for Germany, and for all of Europe. The groundwork for the changes had been laid in June, 1947, when in an address at Harvard University Secretary of State George Marshall stated the intention of the United States to grant economic aid for the restoration of Europe.

Russian opposition to the restoration of Germany under a democratic system of government became evident at a foreign ministers' conference, and the Cold War, that battle of nerves between the Western powers and the Soviet Union, entered a new phase. Russia needed to win Berlin to gain all of Germany, and she gradually exerted more pressure on the Allies.

The Western powers were undecided about the importance of Berlin and a common action, but finally united the German territory under their control. The Soviets protested by walking out of the Allied Control Council. Next the Western powers decided to change the currency then in use and introduced a new Westmark.

But what about Berlin? It was simple to make these changes in the western sectors of Germany, but Berlin lay in the eastern sector, surrounded by the Soviet Zone.

The Allies in Berlin wanted to bring economic independence there too, but suddenly, in the summer of 1948, the Soviets acted. A bridge near Magdeburg had to be repaired, so the streets leading out of Berlin were made temporarily impassable. Then railway traffic, highways and waterways to and from the West were also blocked, leaving open only the three air corridors, each about fifteen miles wide. Berlin was blockaded.

Why did the Russians do it? Did they plan to drive the Western powers out of Berlin? Were they trying to seal off their zone? Did they want to give themselves control of the city? Or were the Russians merely trying to humiliate the West? In any case, the gamble was a good one. A city of 2.4 million people was isolated. Except for the three air corridors, the city had no avenue of supply.

On June 26, Operation Vittles began. Milk for the babies, medicine for the ill, foodstuffs for the aged, all had to be supplied by air. The Western powers were prepared to airlift supplies to the city for an unlimited length of time. It was estimated that to keep Berlin alive required from 3,500 to 4,500 tons of materials daily. Was this possible? The Berliners were skeptical. In a letter to a West German newspaper a Berliner described his shift from doubts, to acceptance, to confidence in victory:

> First day—got to Zehlendorf. Americans still there. Am calmed.
> Tenth day—dried potatoes, dried vegetables, tinned meat, egg powder, I'm still calmer.
> Thirteenth day—coal from the heavens. Planes like clockwork. Earplugs by my bed.

American and British planes flew an average of 1,500 tons of produce to Berlin daily. But everyone wondered what would happen if the blockade persisted into the cold winter months. Could the Berliners survive without fuel for heat or cooking? Ernst Reuter spoke for all Berliners when he answered, "We shall in any case continue on our way. Do what you are able to do, we shall do what we feel to be our duty."

The blockade was a harsh experience for everyone in Berlin. The Brandts were not exempt, but their life was made somewhat easier by parcels sent by their Scandinavian friends. Both Willy and Rut had been accustomed to a spare life, and the blockade merely strengthened their ability to face difficult situations. However, Rut was now expecting the birth of their first child, and Peter was born during the blockade in a poorly heated, candlelit hospital.

But all Berliners were prepared to make whatever sacrifices were necessary. And they did. Throughout the long winter months planes landed, unloaded their vital cargoes, and took off again. On just one day, April 16, 1949, 1,400 planes landed in Berlin's airports—an airplane every sixty-three seconds. They transported 5,300 tons of coal, 1,850 tons of foodstuffs, 1,000 tons of raw materials of different kinds. All that on a single day. Prior to the blockade, it took all the highways and waterways to bring that same amount of cargo to Berlin.

The blockade was lifted on May 4, 1949, exactly 314 days after it began. In those eleven months more than 2 million tons of cargo had been flown into Berlin, a revolutionary statement about air power, about the dedication of the fliers and ground crews, and about the courage of the Berliners themselves.

When "traffic restrictions," as the blockade was called, finally ended, Reuter said the Berliners could celebrate "the most beautiful May since 1945." In one sense, that was true. Berliners were once again free to leave or enter their city. In another sense, however, it was not true. The end of the blockade saw the schism between the East and West more firmly entrenched than ever. The Federal Republic of West Germany and the German Democratic Republic of East Germany had become permanent divisions, and the city of Berlin was split down the middle.

CHAPTER VII

A Career in Politics

Elections were held on August 14, 1949, to choose a president, the ceremonial head of West Germany, and a chancellor, the political head. In a close election, Professor Theodor Heuss was elected federal president, and he proposed Dr. Konrad Adenauer for chancellor. Remarkably enough, the proposal was carried by one vote—Adenauer's own! At the time he was seventy-three years old. Adenauer's government faced the great problems of unemployment, of large numbers of refugees coming from the East Zone, of disruptions of German industry and productivity, and of caring for the many who had been disabled in the war.

Several months later, in December, West Berlin elections took place in spite of Communist disturbances. Of those entitled to vote, 83.9 percent cast their ballots in an open election. Ernst Reuter was then elected lord mayor of Berlin by the Municipal Assembly.

As early as 1945 the Allies had gradually structured Germany into administrative *Länder* (states). Some of these were based on traditional German states, while others were developed to serve the specific needs of the Allies. Eleven states were established in the west, and five in the Soviet Zone. Berlin was organized as a separate state. The existence of these states influenced the drafting of the German constitution later—a constitution that reflected the philosophies of the occupying powers. In the East Zone, for example, all private banks were confiscated and reorganized as state or provincial banks, while in the West Zone, private ownership of banks was continued.

In the two sections of Germany, the bases for two central German governments gradually evolved. In 1947 the Economic Council was created for the West Zone for the purpose of formulating policies on economic matters. Members were selected by proportional representation. In 1948 the Council of States was added, whose members were prime ministers and chief ministers of the individual states. The Economic Council became a preliminary lower house of parliament while the Council of States became a preliminary upper house. A preliminary cabinet, known as the Administrative Council, was created in May, 1947, and the German High Court in February, 1948. German politicians and experts played a large role in setting up these organizations—the beginnings of West German government.

In the Soviet Zone, a Permanent Economic Commission was created by the Russians, its members appointed by the military administration, trade unions, and farmers' organizations. In this procedure of appointing delegates, the Soviets lessened the importance of parliaments and elections.

Once preliminary organizations were formed, it was necessary to draw up a constitution for West Germany. At a meeting on July 1, 1948, the military governors presented the German prime ministers with three documents. The first gave them power to convene an assembly to draft a democratic federal constitution. The second authorized the Germans to investigate boundary changes among the states. The third described the powers reserved by the Allies to aid them in the occupation.

The Parliamentary Council, as the constitution-drafting body was called, drew up the Basic Law (*Grundgesetz*) on

May 8, 1949, locating the temporary capital in Bonn. After the Basic Law was ratified by the states, it became the constitution of Germany. The Basic Law provided for a bicameral system with a popularly elected lower house, the Bundestag, and an upper house, the Bundesrat. Article 1 proclaimed: "Germany is an indivisible democratic republic; its constituent parts are the German states. The Republic decides on all matters essential for the continued existence and development of the German people as a whole." No mention was made of the area in which the constitution was valid. It was assumed that another constitution would be drawn up as soon as Germany was united.

At the time the Basic Law was being drafted, Willy Brandt was the liaison man of the Social Democratic Party executive board. Although he was offered a party office in one of the states for the next election, he turned it down because he did not want to leave Berlin. Instead he gladly accepted the opportunity to be sent to Bonn by the Berlin City Assembly as one of eight Berlin representatives and as a spokesman for the city in the first Bundestag.

At this point in Brandt's career he was more active than ever in the Social Democratic Party. He stayed in close contact with the Berlin organization of the party and still participated as a nonvoting member in its central committee. Nevertheless he was charged with many important tasks. He was given the chairmanship of the local party organization in the Wilmersdorf section of Berlin, and he took over the editorship of the party organ, the *Social Democrat,* in 1949. As Brandt became more and more enmeshed in politics on the federal level as a member of the Bundestag, he decided to run for the Berlin Parliament and was elected a member of the Berlin House of Representatives in December, 1950. Dividing his time, he spent many days in Bonn attending plenary sessions or participating in the discussions of the Social Democrats.

For these trips Brandt had to fly, because travel by train or car through the East Zone would have been dangerous for him. The Russians considered him the chief of the eastern office of the Social Democrats and would have arrested him, although he had never actually filled that office.

Brandt's concerns as a member of the Berlin House of Representatives related to international as well as national problems. He represented the interests of Berlin many times and introduced a motion to have the Federal Law apply to Berlin. In 1952 he succeeded in having the number of Berlin representatives increased from eight to nineteen. Berlin then had greater influence in both the Bundestrat and Bundestag, but it was still not effective in passing laws, since Berlin votes were not counted.

At other times Brandt spoke out forcefully on the value of Berlin to the political future of all Germany. He repeatedly suggested that some of the federal ministries be transferred to Berlin to give the city the importance it deserved and needed. When a preliminary movement did begin on behalf of Berlin as the capital instead of Bonn, Brandt tried to "get as much as possible and as fast as possible." The erection of federal buildings, the completion of universities, and the construction of cultural institutions were among Brandt's accomplishments during this period. In 1957 he published *From Bonn to Berlin,* a book about the successful transfer of some federal ministries from Bonn to Berlin, although Bonn remained the capital of West Germany. The overriding concern, however, was the reunification of Germany. Brandt expressed it this way: "We must awake the satisfied and the tired, the lazy and complacent, and never stop asking ourselves whether the German policy has really done all it could do to concentrate all the forces of our nation on one decisive point and to impel the people with a boundless will to win the struggle for the reunification of Germany."

Germany was more than ever divided into two zones, East and West, and Berlin lay inside the East Zone like a pearl between the halves of an oyster shell. How could all Germany be reunited under one governing body? How could all the people of Germany take part in general elections? How could the people of Berlin move freely in and out of their city? These questions plagued Brandt.

They also plagued the people of East Germany, especially those of East Berlin. On June 16, 1953, about eighty building workers in East Berlin went on strike against the higher work quotas that had been imposed upon them by the Soviets. Carrying a red sign with the slogan, "We demand a reduction of norms," workers marched to the central office of the Free Trade Union Federation. As they marched through the streets, others joined them. Soon more than two thousand men were shouting, "Mates, join us, this is the beginning!" Although the group was chiefly concerned with economic problems, some of them demanded resignation of the government and free elections.

The next day strikes and demonstrations took place all over East Germany. In some places they were orderly and peaceful, in others disruptful and dangerous. Early in the morning of the seventeenth, Russian armored cars and tanks were patrolling the streets. Shots were fired, and twenty-one people were killed. Before the People's Revolt, as it was to be known, was over, 372,000 workers had put down their tools, and not until late in the evening did the crowds disperse and peace slowly return. But the revolt had been partially successful, for work quotas were reduced, and some of the workers' economic and social demands were considered in the following months.

The seventeenth of June became the official "Day of German Unity" as proclaimed by the Bundestag on July 1, 1953. On that occasion Brandt addressed the Bundestag:

"The struggle for a reunification in freedom has the precedence of all plans and projects in foreign affairs. We will not make any progress with the hesitation and timidity of those who apparently fear nothing more than the possibility that their own cherished plans might be discarded by a successful policy of reunification.

"The workers in the zone have recognized the moment when spontaneous actions could be started. Now it is our task in the Western World to recognize the moment when the German question can—if at all—be solved on an international level. Of course, no one of us is foolish enough to declare that a positive result is certain. We are armed with skepticism. But in spite of skepticism and distrust we believe that negotiations ought to be attempted, and the attempt has to be made quickly.

"There is no other solution than the peaceful solution of the German problem. There is no other possibility than to negotiate about the German question. We demand more activity, more clarity, more determination in the fight for German unity in peace and freedom."

Brandt hoped the June 17 uprising would give the Allies additional clout to pressure the Russians into unifying the two Germanies; it did not. The Allies seemed to care more

A Career in Politics

about proving they were not responsible for the East German uprising. Their passivity gave the Russians the advantage, and Germany remained split.

Brandt got another shock on September 29 of that year, when Ernst Reuter died. The death of the lord mayor was a blow to all of Berlin. As Brandt walked home from Reuter's house, he saw an unforgettable sight. In street after street, in every window of every apartment and house, a candle was burning. Reuter had asked the people of Berlin one Christmas to put candles in their windows as a greeting for all those they did not want to forget, both in the East Zone and all over the world. Now the people of Berlin had done the same thing for him as a warm expression of their grief.

Brandt's career continued to develop, both in the party and in national politics. When the second Bundestag met in August, 1953, he was made a member of the Executive Committee of the Social Democratic Parliamentary Group. He gradually built a following of supporters, and in 1954 ran for chairman of the Berlin organization of the party. Defeated by only two votes, he became vice chairman. Then in December, 1954, Brandt was elected president of the Berlin House of Representatives. The position was a prestigious one and offered the opportunity to work beyond the party. Brandt had now, at the age of forty-one, reached such stature in the party that he was being compared favorably with Ernst Reuter.

Then in 1956 the new lord mayor of Berlin, Otto Suhr, in the first year of his term of office, became afflicted with a serious illness, and immediately Brandt was named his potential successor. The post was not one he had aspired to. Rather, Brandt preferred to serve Berlin in a Federal capacity.

Brandt's reserve of personal strength met a very real challenge in November, 1956, when the Communist oppression in Hungary caused the people to revolt. The West German reaction to this was a mass demonstration, partly in sympathy for the Hungarians and partly for the East Germans who three years before had been through the same experience. Nearly a hundred thousand people gathered in front of Schoneberg City Hall. The speakers could scarcely be heard above the calls for action.

"To Brandenburg Gate!" "To the Soviet Embassy!" "Russians go home!" were the cries from all sides.

Brandt mounted the platform. Although he had not been on the program, he was permitted to speak. He reminded the crowd of the responsibility of the United Nations. He warned that cries of indignation would not help. He correctly appraised the tenor of the crowd and feared a march on the East sector.

"Come with me," he urged the crowd, "to the Steinplatz and stage your demonstration there in front of the memorial for the victims of Stalinism."

Many demonstrators followed Brandt while others went home, but another group of several thousand marched, carrying torches, to the Brandenburg Gate, where the West German police tried to stop them. Every minute the situation became more dangerous. Brandt felt that somehow he had to prevent the worst possible demonstrations—bloody clashes on the border of the Russian sector. There, any fight would involve not only the demonstrators and the West German police, but also the East German People's Police and Russian tanks. Any shooting could mean war.

A Career in Politics

Brandt and his wife Rut drove to the critical spot. Brandt jumped out of the car, ran to a police riot car, seized a microphone, and addressed the crowd, mostly students and other youth. He told them that they were playing into Russian hands by fighting among themselves.

Meanwhile, Rut directed a cadre of students in calming the crowd. Gradually the two of them, Willy and Rut, brought the crowd under control and succeeded in ending the fighting by leading the group in singing "Good Comrade"—the same group that a few minutes before had been at each other's throats.

At that moment Brandt received word of another outbreak of violence. Driving at once to the site, he found that the police had begun to disperse the crowd. Brandt climbed on top of a car and again entreated the crowd to remember that shooting and violence could only provoke a war. Again he succeeded in getting the crowd to sing, this time the German national anthem.

After the crowd had dispersed, Brandt and Rut sat with a few friends in his office. They felt no heroism for having diverted a potentially dangerous situation—only relief that they had been able to help Berliners in a moment of crisis. Nevertheless, in their modest, courageous way, they had won the hearts of the city.

Several months before Brandt became lord mayor, his political rivals viciously attacked and slandered him for emigrating to Norway during Hitler's time. They even twisted the contents of a historical study he had written, *Guerillakriget,* in a smear campaign against him, interpreting the book as "advice on how to murder hundreds of thousands of German soldiers." Brandt defended himself openly in a civil suit, using the opportunity to explain the motives for his wartime decisions.

Finally, in late August, 1957, Brandt received notice suddenly that Otto Suhr was dying. After Suhr's death, with the support of great numbers of Berliners, Brandt's party unanimously nominated and elected him to the position of lord mayor of Berlin. This post, which Brandt held for nearly ten years, was the most important one in Germany outside the Federal Administration in Bonn. In it Brandt faced no ordinary task.

That same year, 1957, Adenauer's Christian Democratic Party (CDU/CSU) defeated the Social Democratic Party for the third straight time in national elections. Although Brandt's party, the Social Democrats, gained slightly at the polls (from 28.8 percent to 31.8 percent), the Christian Democrats achieved a smashing victory of 50 percent, making them the first political party in the history of Germany to win a plurality of the votes. Of the 497 Bundestag seats, Adenauer's CDU/CSU party took 270 seats, compared to the SPD's 169. The Socialists were in disarray, and many of their leaders argued that a major overhaul was needed in the party.

Brandt, a strong exponent of the "reformist line," offered himself as a candidate for chairman of the party in 1958. He was defeated in his bid but was elected instead to the executive committee. Then, at the party's Bad Godesberg convention in 1959, the SPD passed a new program, one that marked a major change in its political platform and leadership.

The preamble to their program declared that Democratic socialism was not a rival of religion but was based on Christian ethics, humanism, and classic philosophy. The SPD stood for freedom of the mind and for the right of all to have individual beliefs and opinions. In foreign policy, the program endorsed the principle of national defense, NATO, the foundation of the European Common Market, the unification of Germany, and European integration. It rejected the manufacturing of nuclear weapons by the Federal Republic and called for a general ban against such weapons.

In domestic policies, the program advocated full employment, a stable currency, and widespread economic and social reforms. The Socialist concept of nationalizing some industry was dropped as the program called for a "planning policy related to the economic cycle." But it stressed that "free competition and free enterprise are important elements of its policy."

The new motto of the SPD was, "As much competition as possible, as much planning as necessary." The program declared that "the SPD, which was a party of the working class, is now a party of the whole people."

The new program rejected the old Socialist dream of some future utopia based on Marxian philosophy. Instead it pointed to a more realistic goal. As Brandt said of the program, "New demands are on the agenda, new reforms will follow. They will usher in either a paradise on earth or a boring conformity. But they will bring us a more harmonious social order, a constitutional state which will become more and more a social and cultural state. This is more than a program for a day, this is a goal towards which we must continually strive."

Along with the Bad Godesberg program, the Social Democratic Party picked a new team of leaders headed by Willy Brandt. The reformers had insisted that the image of the party in the eyes of the German voters was a poor one—too old, too somber, and too dull. Brandt was just the opposite. He, like John Kennedy in America, projected a youthful, handsome, likable image, and he had a pretty and intelligent wife.

The reformers of the SPD also learned from their election technique mistakes. In 1957, while the opposition was hiring market-research specialists to determine what colors were most attractive on billboards and what slogans had the most punch with the voters, the SPD relied on its "poor but honest" image to win the voters' hearts. They displayed somber posters with dull-yellow lettering on a black background, and published unflattering cartoons of their leader Ollenhauer. All that changed as Brandt and his new team emphasized more attractive electioneering with a big push for more television and radio campaigning.

Brandt's advisers consisted of Karl Schiller, Fritz Erler, Helmut Schmidt, and Herbert Wehner, all of them about Brandt's age. They were leaders faithful to the party's traditional style and tone, and all were specialists.

Wehner, who handled party affairs, was the son of a cobbler and had earlier been a Communist Party member, but he had broken with the Communists during a long exile in Russia and Sweden from 1935 to 1946. It was he, in particular, who argued that the SPD had to convince the nonworking classes that the party could rule responsibly.

Schmidt and Schiller were from middle-class families and were well educated. Schmidt became an expert in defense affairs, while Schiller, an economist, handled budget and fiscal matters.

Erler, a man of character and intelligence, was the party's foreign-affairs specialist, but his health had been broken during long years in prison under the Nazis, and he died prematurely in 1967.

Brandt's team of supporters geared up for the 1961

national election. With a fresh platform, dynamic new leaders, and youthful confidence they prepared to do battle with that sly old political fox, Konrad Adenauer.

Adenauer had dominated German politics since the founding of the Federal Republic in 1949, but by the late 1950's he seemed to be losing his political touch. He toyed with the thought of running for President in 1959, but suddenly dropped the idea when he realized how much his power would be reduced in that largely ceremonial post. His often authoritarian style of running the government also irritated many, and his progress toward German unification seemed nonexistent. Then too, the eighty-five-year-old Adenauer appeared to be out of step with the times. In the United States the young John Kennedy had been elected President in 1960, and it was obvious that Kennedy and Adenauer would find it difficult to work together as closely as Adenauer had with the former President Eisenhower and his Secretary of State, John Foster Dulles.

Brandt conducted a whirlwind campaign in 1961, a German copy of Kennedy's successful presidential campaign the year before. "Smiling Willy," seen everywhere, was a charming, youthful contrast to the old chancellor. Nearly every city and hamlet in West Germany saw him. Racing at breakneck speed around the country, he delivered twenty or thirty short talks a day, hammering away at the issues: the lack of progress on German unification, the Berlin problem, the need for social and economic reforms, the growing problems of the cities, and the need for fresh leadership. Most of all, Brandt wanted to present himself and his party as a dynamic team that could meet the problems of a new generation.

Privately Brandt realized that it was virtually impossible to overturn Adenauer, but he felt that he was building a case for the 1965 elections. Too many German voters saw Adenauer as the grand wizard of politics. He was already being compared to the great Bismarck, and there was no denying his accomplishments. Germany had not only recovered from the war but was prospering. Germany was also respected and trusted by her allies; she had returned to the fold of international respectability. Many Germans could rationalize their vote for Adenauer by saying, "In fact, I don't particularly like him, but I can't imagine how things would go if he were not there." Adenauer's campaign slogan, *"Sicher ist sicher"* ("Sure is sure"), played on this idea. But the SPD answered with their own slogan based on a popular gasoline commercial, "Put a Willy in the tank."

The 1961 election was a hard one and perhaps the dirtiest campaign in recent times. The CDU made a national issue of Brandt's illegitimate birth and his years in exile. Even Adenauer made a comment in a public address about "Brandt alias Frahm," while his henchmen did much more. "Where was Brandt in 1944? In Safety!" was written on banners towed by two airplanes during the election campaign. But Brandt asserted that he had never chosen the easy way out. "And yet," he said, "I must appear to many as an extreme case: two changes of citizenship, not both willingly, but still two; a change of name—as a protection against persecution and then as a matter of conviction, but still a change; the resolution of a young radical left-wing Socialist—who becomes chairman of the Social Democrats, perhaps the biggest change of all." Although Brandt showed great strength in the face of the bitter attacks, he was deeply hurt, both for himself and for his family. He was, at the same time, facing the great stresses of the Berlin Wall and had limited his campaigning so that he could devote his energies to his city.

For his efforts on behalf of Berlin and its thousands of devoted inhabitants, Brandt won the American Freedom House Award, but he lost the chancellorship. On September 17, 1961, as the results of the election came in, it was obvious that the SPD had improved its position. Nearly 11.5 million Germans had voted for them, 2 million more than in 1957, and their vote rose from 31.8 percent to 36.3 percent. But it was not enough; Adenauer had won again.

The election of 1961 was a partial setback for Brandt, but at least he had won his spurs in national politics. He was criticized for patterning his campaign too much on the Kennedy campaign and not enough on his own style. Brandt took the criticism, studied the results, and aimed for the next election for chancellor in 1965.

CHAPTER VIII

Warrior for Berlin

West Berlin's 125 square miles were situated 110 miles inside East Germany, the German Democratic Republic. Its 2.2 million inhabitants made it the largest and most important city in all of Germany. At the height of the Cold War, the former capital city of Germany was as much an international pressure point as Hong Kong was in the Far East. Here in Berlin the two superpowers in the Cold War met "eyeball to eyeball"; here in Berlin two different life-styles and ideologies met in daily competition. As a result, Berliners felt themselves in the center of world events—*eine Weltstadt* (a world city) they fondly called their city.

Berlin has never had the special relationship with the rest of the Germans that Paris has for the French or London for the English. Berlin was always the saucy upstart, the city that grew up too fast. A youngster of a town by most European standards, the city was founded in the thirteenth century. It was the capital of Prussia, but many southern Germans felt that it had never been one of the great historical German cities, such as Munich, Hamburg, Frankfurt, or Cologne. All of this had changed in the last hundred years, as Berlin grew into the largest, most industrial city in Germany, the center of its political, financial, and cultural life. Then, when Germany was united in 1871, Berlin became the capital.

The Berliners' life-style was formed in these years too,

and it was a style that was not typically German. Berliners were reputed to be too witty, Berlin girls too pretty, Berlin students too extreme, Berlin humor too quick, Berlin business too hard-boiled, and Berlin tempo too fast. Berlin was the place where the young went to conquer the world, and Willy Brandt was no exception. Berlin always had room for the energetic and the talented. It soon accepted Lord Mayor Brandt as one of its own.

The city had suffered terribly from World War II. Nearly one fifth of all the rubble in Germany was located in the Greater Berlin area. In West Berlin alone, 73 million cubic yards of debris had to be cleared away. Most of the rubble was piled into low hills, sodded over, and made into parks, which have since become the favorite skiing and sled-riding slopes of the younger Berliners.

The city planners sought to combine reconstruction and urban renewal, but what a task they had! One systematic town plan was superseded by another. Then, in 1957 under Brandt, the Berlin Senate launched the Berlin-Capital City competition, which stressed the construction of large-scale public buildings in a variety of styles to form economic and cultural centers throughout the city. The most successful example of reconstruction was in the bombed-out Hansa Quarter, a residential area that was the subject of a model program undertaken by architects from fourteen different countries. The quarter became a center for innovations in housing.

These model programs of reconstruction were seen by writers and artists, as well as the residents of the city, as signs of strength and beauty. Christoph Meckel, the poet, could have been writing about the rebirth of Berlin when he wrote "The Peacock":

> I saw no phoenix mount from Germany's ashes.
> Rummaging in the ash with my foot
> I turned up charred fins, horns and sloughs—
> yet I saw a peacock, swirling up the ash
> with one wing of wood and the other of iron,
> growing enormous, and he whipped
> at the flakes where the burning had been
> and he fanned out his plumage.

West Berlin was, and still is, more like a small country than a city. It has ninety-four towns, villages, and communes, two airports, forty-three railroad stations, thirteen municipal docks, 1,700 miles of roads, 400,000 cars, a million apartments and 6,000 bars! Despite the blockade and other harassment by the East Germans West Berlin generally shared in the "economic miracle" of German recovery. New buildings sprang up, industries revived, and unemployment disappeared. Marshall Plan aid of nearly $1 billion and heavy subsidies from Bonn did much to stimulate Berlin's economy. By 1957, when Brandt became mayor, the West Berlin shops bulged with goods, and the newly built apartments and streets concealed the destruction wrought by the war. The dramatic differences between the abundance of West Berlin and the shabbiness of East Berlin were clearly visible to all. And that was the problem.

Berlin was a show city for Western affluence, a center for Western information to the peoples of Eastern Europe, and a perpetual thorn in the side of the Soviet Union and her Eastern European satellites. Daily from the radio and television transmitters of West Berlin came the Western version of the Cold War to millions of viewers and listeners behind the Iron Curtain. Millions more visited West Berlin for a firsthand look at the Western world. Eastern Europeans traveled to East Berlin and then took the elevated train or subway to West Berlin.

The Federal Republic of Germany encouraged this flow of visitors to West Berlin by allowing East Germans to buy many goods and services at the exchange rate of one East German mark to one West German mark, although the usual rate of exchange was 4 to 1. Special music programs were scheduled in West Berlin, especially jazz and rock groups, which at that time were forbidden behind the Iron Curtain, to entice visitors from the East. Art shows, football matches, political meetings, and business conventions were sent to Berlin to encourage the East Germans to maintain their contacts with their Western brothers, and also to sell the Western way of life to the East.

There was undoubtedly a strong streak of propaganda in the activities of the Western powers in West Berlin in this period, but the propaganda from East Germany was even more shrill in its attacks on the West. It was the height of the Cold War, and propaganda from both sides was overdone.

The most significant and damaging aspect of West Berlin's presence deep inside East Germany was the unending stream of refugees. From the end of World War II to 1974 nearly 4 million Germans left East Germany for the West. From 1949, when detailed records were first kept, to 1961, when the Berlin Wall was built, 2,732,734 people became refugees to West Berlin and the Federal Republic rather than live under a regime they disliked in the East. Millions of Germans voluntarily chose the risks, uncertainties, and hardships of a refugee's life rather than stay in East Germany.

Some refugees left the East to rejoin parts of their family in the West, some left because of religious or political reasons, but most left because they wanted a better way of life. From 1945 to 1961 nearly 20 percent of the total population of East Germany left, mostly through West Berlin. The flow rose sharply during tension-filled periods, such as in 1953 at the time of the East German riots, or in 1956 at the time of the Hungarian uprisings, but month after month a steady stream of refugees who "voted with their feet" moved west. Significantly, about half of these refugees were under twenty-five years old, and a high percentage were skilled men and women in all fields: doctors, engineers, dental technicians, draftsmen, metalworkers, miners, farmers, and teachers. They were just the kind of people the East German regime could ill afford to lose.

Naturally the mass flight disturbed the East German authorities. They stepped up their indoctrination and imposed stricter measures to stem the flow. Anyone who was caught trying to escape was subject to imprisonment, and relatives left behind were liable to retaliation. A border zone of watchtowers, mined fields, and barbed-wire fences was built and manned by heavily armed troops of the People's Police. But nothing could stop the human hemorrhage from East Germany. The very existence of the regime was threatened by this steady drain on its most precious resource—human labor. Economic goals could not be fulfilled, universities staffed, or political programs carried out until the drain of human beings was stopped.

Besides the refugee crisis, the East German government linked West Berlin to the other difficulties that grew out of World War II, and blamed it for the German unification problem, poor East–West relationships, and the possibility of a future united Europe. Berlin became a key symbol in contemporary politics, a crucial factor in the

Cold War. As Willy Brandt noted, Berlin "has a decisive bearing upon the future of the whole of Germany. One can state it simply: what is good for Berlin is also good for Germany."

After the failure of the Berlin Blockade of 1948–1949, the Soviet leaders changed their tactics on the Berlin issue. Their goals were still the same; they wanted to force the Western powers out of West Berlin, consolidate East Germany, force the recognition of East Germany, and split West Germany from the other Western bloc countries. Berlin became a convenient issue to use in applying political pressure on the Western powers. From 1949 to 1958 the Soviets used a series of harassments against Berlin. Their constant meddling in the transport and delivery of goods from the West was accompanied by a violent propaganda campaign designed to intimidate West Berliners and undermine Allied occupation rights.

Although a number of international conferences were held on the German question and Berlin, all ended in a stalemate. The Western powers' formula of German unification via free and open elections was unacceptable to the Soviets, who insisted on unification through negotiations between the "two German states." The lines between the two German states hardened still more when West Germany joined the North Atlantic Treaty Organization in 1955 and East Germany joined the Warsaw Pact. Two years later West Germany became one of the original members of the Common Market, while East Germany joined the Russian-controlled Council for Mutual Economic Assistance.

The status of Berlin in all these negotiations was somewhat ambiguous. The Western powers insisted that Berlin was still a Four Power–occupied city, while the Russians insisted that East Berlin was the legitimate capital of East Germany and that *only* West Berlin was occupied. In effect, the Russians sought to present Germany as divided into three parts: West Germany, East Germany, and West Berlin. Western authorities ignored this interpretation by continually making their presence known in Berlin, as well as by regularly protesting any violation of the many agreements made over it.

The West German position on Berlin was that it was a part of West Germany under military occupation. Laws passed by the West German parliament were not effective in West Berlin unless approved by the Berlin senate and the Allied military authorities. West Berliners could not be drafted into their army, nor were representatives of West Berlin officially allowed to vote in the parliament. Willy Brandt, for example, was one of the Berlin representatives to the Bonn parliament. He voted and participated in debate and committee work but officially his status was that of a nonvoting member.

The East German position was simple: Berlin belonged to the East German state and the Western occupation of West Berlin must be terminated. The Russians and their East German allies followed a pattern of piecemeal attacks at western occupational rights in Berlin. Willy Brandt labeled them "salami tactics," or attempts to whittle down former rights gradually.

In November, 1958, a little over a year after Brandt became mayor, these salami tactics came to an abrupt halt as the Russians precipitated the second Berlin crisis. On November 10, Nikita S. Khrushchev, Premier and party chief of the Soviet Union, publicly denounced the Potsdam agreements, especially those parts pertaining to the Four Power status of Berlin. On November 27, he sent notes to the Western powers and the Federal Republic that he would "cancel all commitments on Berlin" in six months. He summarily demanded the withdrawal of all Western forces from the city and the abolition of all ties existing between Berlin and the Federal Republic.

Khrushchev proposed turning Berlin into a "free city" until such time that Germany could be united. He suggested that the two parts of Germany negotiate for a confederation to recognize the East German regime, but he did not mention elections. If his demands were not met, the Soviet government threatened, it would sign a peace treaty with East Germany giving it physical control of Berlin, including Western access rights to the city.

Khrushchev's note ignored the fact that the presence of the Four Powers in Berlin was rooted not in negotiations between them but in their original rights as occupants of a defeated Germany. Moreover, he was ignoring the general rules of international law that treaty rights based on negotiations and occupation arrangements cannot be unilaterally modified.

Khrushchev's Berlin crisis of 1958, only one year after Brandt became mayor, changed Brandt from a little-known ambitious young politician to an internationally known leader. People around the world soon became accustomed to hearing about the courageous young mayor of the beleaguered city of Berlin. And they liked what they heard.

Brandt and his wife traveled halfway around the world to plead the case for Berlin. Their tour of the United States was especially successful, as Brandt's sincerity, charm, and naturalness made a great impression on the American public. In television programs like *Meet the*

Press and in countless interviews, Brandt, in his slow but excellent English, explained to Americans the real issues involved in West Berlin's existence.

Brandt pleaded the case of West Berlin before the United Nations and before world opinion at every opportunity. His critics at home accused him of aspiring to dictate foreign policy for West Germany, and indeed, it was sometimes difficult to remember that the Federal Republic was responsible for Berlin. But Brandt had a dramatic appeal. Unlike Chancellor Adenauer, he captured people's imagination. That is why millions of New Yorkers braved the rain and snow on February 10, 1959, to shout their encouragement as, showered by ticker tape, he slowly drove up Broadway to City Hall. Brandt was easily the most popular German politician America had known for a long time.

Despite the demanding schedule of meetings, speeches, greeting prominent visitors to Berlin, and traveling throughout West Germany and the world to rally support for his beloved city, Brandt still found some time to carry on in West Berlin the work of reconstruction, improvement of education, and encouragement of industrial production.

Nevertheless, his regular duties as mayor had to take second place to the responsibility of coping with the international crisis. After the first Khrushchev note, there had been some panicky selling of real estate, and a few businesses had moved out of the city, but Brandt never wavered. He quickly arranged a meeting with influential businessmen from West Germany and convinced them that Berlin had a future. Within a few months many new orders poured into Berlin factories, and a possible economic crisis was averted.

In 1958 Brandt had won the elections in the city handily. He had also been named chairman of the Socialist Party in Berlin. Unlike the Socialists in most parts of West Germany, Brandt decided to collaborate with Berlin's Christian Democratic Party (CDU) so they could present a united front to the Soviets. When the Berlin crisis began later, this united front was of great importance to him, because it enabled him to speak with a mandate from an overwhelming majority of Berliners.

Brandt was actually much closer to Adenauer's view of foreign policy than most of his fellow Socialists. He understood the need for a determined stand against Soviet pressure and resolved to carry the word throughout the world that Berlin would not surrender but was determined to defend its right to live. The man and his city's fight for freedom became inseparable; they were a symbol of freedom in the midst of the Cold War.

The crisis of Berlin threatened the world with nuclear war. Despite threats and counterthreats, interspersed with demands for a new summit meeting, the machinery of diplomacy slowly ground out a solution. After a round of top-level meetings among the Western leaders, Prime Minister Harold Macmillan of England visited Moscow. Finally Premier Khrushchev withdrew his six-month deadline, while the powers arranged a foreign ministers' conference in Geneva to discuss Germany and the Berlin problems.

In May and June, 1959, thirty-one meetings of the ministers were held, but no agreement was reached except on a few minor points. The Russians left Geneva still determined to subdue Berlin. Their threat was not withdrawn, just postponed. The Western nations had held fast, but they were prepared to begin summit meeting negotiations with the Russians over Berlin as a separate issue if need be.

The planned summit conference was to be held in Paris on May 16, 1960, but barely three hours after it opened Khrushchev terminated it, citing as his reasons the U-2 incident—that is, the downing of an American high-altitude reconnaissance plane deep inside Russia—and the failure of the Geneva disarmament talks. Throughout the rest of the year, the Soviets continued to demand that Berlin be discussed independently from the general German unification issue.

Brandt rejected this Soviet line of reasoning as foolish. German unification was not only a German national problem, but also a problem of East–West relations. To Khrushchev's thesis that the unification of Germany was "up to the Germans themselves," Brandt answered: "Look at the people of Berlin and you will know what the Germans want! The day will come when the Brandenburg Gate will no longer be situated at our border. Until that day comes we beg, appeal, demand: *Macht die Tür auf!* Open the door! End the unnatural division! We declare solemnly: the right of self-determination must also be granted to the Germans. The brutal intervention in the inner affairs of our people cannot be tolerated indefinitely. At a time when the colonial rule in other parts of the world is being abolished, we cannot tolerate a new colonialism in the heart of Europe."

Early in 1961 Khrushchev again implied that he was determined to settle the Berlin issue. "Berlin sticks in our throats like a rat," he said, and he quickly applied pressure on the newly installed Kennedy administration. The time seemed right; there was obvious discord among the Western powers over the negotiations with the East.

France's de Gaulle and Germany's Adenauer were far more rigid than England's Macmillan or America's Kennedy. The position of the young President of the United States was crucial.

Brandt had met Kennedy once before his election, but on March 16, 1961, he had a long interview with the recently inaugurated President. Brandt reported on the growing economic strength of Berlin and on the great confidence the Berliners had in America and its government. Brandt stressed to the President that Soviet policy was not only directed against the people of West Berlin, but also at American prestige, credibility, and confidence. America had as much at stake in Berlin as did West Germany.

Kennedy left no doubt in Brandt's mind that the United States was determined to guarantee Berlin's freedom. In the late spring he made his first presidential trip to Europe to confer with General de Gaulle and Prime Minister Macmillan. Then on June 3 he met Khrushchev in Vienna. The meeting between the heads of the two most powerful nations in the world was cool, courteous, and serious. They made no progress on the German or Berlin issues and disarmament, and just before they adjourned, Khrushchev announced rather harshly that his decision to sign a separate peace treaty with East Germany by December still stood. Kennedy replied, "If that is true, we shall have a cold winter."

Another crisis seemed unavoidable. The Soviet Union's military budget was increased and hints were made about actions against the "outlaw city."

Kennedy replied to Soviet threats in a very serious tone on July 25. "West Berlin . . . has many roles. It is more than a showcase of liberty, a symbol, an island of freedom in a Communist sea. It is even more than a link with the Free World, a beacon of hope behind the Iron Curtain, an escape hatch for refugees. West Berlin is all of that. But above all, it has now become—as never before—the great testing place of Western courage and will, a focal point where our solemn commitments stretching back over the years since 1945 and Soviet ambitions now meet in basic confrontation."

In the midst of the struggle over Berlin, Brandt faced opponent Konrad Adenauer in another battle for the chancellorship. In the public eye their bitter clash in the press was second only to an ominous international crisis.

Meanwhile, the stream of refugees into West Berlin mounted to flood proportions—20,000 in June, 30,000 in July, and nearly 17,000 in the first twelve days of August. West Berlin was taking in almost 2,500 refugees a day. Campaigning in West Germany, Brandt wondered aloud, "What is causing so many East Germans to give up their homes? Why are so many people fleeing to West Germany? What is causing their anxiety?"

He did not have long to wait for answers. At midnight, August 13, 1961, the East German army and the People's Police began encircling the entire perimeter of West Berlin with barbed wire. Within days the wire was replaced by a wall of solid cement blocks, topped with broken glass and more barbed wire.

With the first news of the Berlin Wall, Brandt broke off his campaigning and immediately took a plane to Berlin. "For me there isn't any more election, there is just the battle for Berlin." At best, he could devote only one day a week to the campaign as he now defended his city against Soviet threats.

After an inspection of the Wall, Brandt conferred with

the three Western commandants. He began by icily stating, "You let yourselves be kicked in the behind by Ulbricht [East German leader] last night." He wanted to know what they intended to do.

Silence followed. There were no orders to do anything about the Wall.

Two days later Brandt wrote a personal appeal to President Kennedy, arguing that the gravest problem was a crisis of confidence in the Western powers. Kennedy responded by dispatching more military units to Germany and Berlin and by sending his personal envoy, Vice President Lyndon Johnson, to West Berlin. It was clear that the West intended to defend Berlin, but it was equally clear that it did not, or would not, do anything about the Wall.

The situation in Berlin simmered as escapees tunneled, vaulted, or smashed their way to freedom. Moments of high tension occurred when American and Russian tanks stood menacingly gun barrel to gun barrel at Checkpoint Charlie, one of the few crossing points in the Wall. The Communist People's Police and the West Berlin police exchanged gunfire during attempted escapes by refugees, but more serious fighting did not occur. Both sides were determined not to let the Berlin crisis escalate into World War III.

For Brandt these were heartrending days as he tried desperately to keep up morale in the city and prevent any rash movements that might provoke a major confrontation with the Soviets. People around the world daily saw unforgettable pictures of East Germans of every age jumping from four- and five-story buildings or from roofs, often to certain death, to flee from the East. Others tried to swim the River Spree or to vault the barbed wire; many died trying to get to the Western sector and freedom.

Despite the seeming differences in the Western powers' camp, they remained firm in the face of the Russian threat to Berlin. In repeated public statements Khrushchev called for the normalization of the status of Berlin under United Nations control and a general peace settlement with Germany, but he refrained from setting any new deadlines.

As for the West Berliners, after the first touch of panic, they settled down to a grudging acceptance of this hideous and visible division of their city. A steady stream of visitors from all over the world came to see the Wall. Seven days after it was started, Vice President Lyndon Johnson viewed the Wall, and in February, 1962, Robert Kennedy, the President's brother, who was the Attorney General of the United States, flew to Berlin to see the great dividing line. Robert Kennedy remarked, "This Wall is an admission of failure for the Communists. This is the first time in human history that such a wall has been erected —not to keep bandits and thieves out, but to keep the populace in prison. The world will understand this."

Soviet intentions after the Wall were difficult to understand. The Wall helped to consolidate the tottering East German state, for now its citizens realized that there was no easy escape. They had to come to grips emotionally with the idea of building their lives in the East German state. Although the Wall was an embarrassment for the Russians, it offered them a chance to pressure the West anytime they chose.

There is some evidence to suggest that in the fall of 1962 the Soviet leaders were planning further actions against Berlin, but that these actions were interrupted by the dangerous Cuban missile crisis. The Russians had tried to establish offensive missile bases in Cuba, but the United States rejected this as a deliberately provocative and unreasonable change in the international status quo. For a few tense days the world stood at the brink of war, but finally the two superpowers resolved the issue. After the Cuban crisis East–West relations improved with the signing of a Test Ban Treaty and the resumption of disarmament talks. No further pressure was applied to Berlin, but the access routes to the city were still a source of continuing discussion.

Early in 1963 Brandt led his Social Democratic Party to a smashing victory in the Berlin elections. His party polled 62 percent of the votes, a resounding vote of confidence from the Berliners for their mayor who had led them through a crisis.

President Kennedy was among those who sent congratulations, and Brandt took this opportunity to remind the President that he had an invitation to visit Berlin. Kennedy was already planning a trip to Europe to demonstrate Western unity, so Berlin was included on his itinerary. In late June, Kennedy visited West Germany and received a tumultuous reception. On June 25 he delivered his major German address at St. Paul's Cathedral in Frankfurt, a shrine of democracy where the first constitution for Germany was written in 1848. Kennedy called for an Atlantic partnership between the Old World and the New World based on a system of cooperation, interdependence, and harmony. The bold words from the young, handsome President impressed even the most cynical Europeans.

But the greatest day of Kennedy's trip was his visit to

West Berlin. It was Berlin's great day, too, for as Brandt wrote, "It is not easy to describe those hours of June 26, 1963, when millions showed their love for John F. Kennedy—when a river flowed through the ancient capital—a river of enthusiasm and gratitude."

Deeply moved by the jubilant, elated crowd around him, the President traveled to Checkpoint Charlie to view the Wall. Silently he gazed across that ugly barrier at the other Berliners, many hundreds of whom had gathered on the east side to catch a glimpse of him. Then briskly he descended from the platform to shake the hands of the West Berliners. He admired them, for he found in them a quality he particularly liked—courage.

Kennedy's major address in Berlin was in front of the City Hall in Schoneberg; it was an address that will long be remembered by Brandt and the citizens of Berlin.

"Two thousand years ago," began the President, "the proudest boast was *civis Romanus sum*. (I am a Roman citizen.) Today, in the world of freedom, the proudest boast is *Ich bin ein Berliner*. (I am a Berliner.)

"There are many people in the world who really don't understand, or say they don't know what the great issue between the Free World and the Communist world is. Let them come to Berlin. There are some who say that Communism is the wave of the future. Let them come to Berlin. And there are some who say in Europe and elsewhere we can work with the Communists. Let them come to Berlin. And there are even a few who say that it is true that Communism is an evil system, but it permits us to make economic progress. *Lass' sie nach Berlin kommen*. Let them come to Berlin. . . .

"Freedom is indivisible, and when one man is enslaved, all are not free. When all are free, then we can look forward to that day when this city will be joined as one and this country and this great continent of Europe in a peaceful and hopeful globe. When that day finally comes, as it will, the people of West Berlin can take sober satisfaction in the fact that they were in the front lines for almost two decades.

"All free men, wherever they may live, are citizens of Berlin, and therefore, as a free man, I take pride in the words *Ich bin ein Berliner*."

Willy Brandt thanked the President on behalf of the millions of Berliners by saying, "This is a great day in the history of our city. We have lived through bad times, and for that very reason, we shall never forget, Mr. President, that you are here with us today and that you addressed us this day."

After a triumphant journey from the City Hall to the Free University, where Kennedy was given an honorary citizenship of Berlin, the President went to the airfield. Before departing he told the German people, "I said yesterday that I was going to leave a note for my successor which would say, 'To be opened at a time of some discouragement.' and in it would be written three words: 'Go to Germany.' I may open that note myself some day."

President Kennedy never would open that note, for within the year he was cut down by an assassin's bullet.

The world mourned; ninety-two delegations from almost every country of the globe, including sixteen presidents and heads of state, accompanied Kennedy on his last journey to Arlington Cemetery. Although not entitled to an invitation to the funeral by diplomatic protocol, Brandt was personally invited by President Johnson.

After attending the funeral and paying his official condolences, word came to him from the widow of President

Kennedy asking if he could pay the family a visit. Jacqueline Kennedy and the President's closest relatives met and spoke with Brandt. Then Robert Kennedy, Mrs. Kennedy, and Brandt went to another room where they sat and talked. Mrs. Kennedy related how full of enthusiasm the President had been after his visit to Germany and especially to Berlin. Brandt told her about the tremendous outburst of mourning that had taken place in Berlin and how Berlin wanted to rename some of its schools and streets for the President. This pleased Mrs. Kennedy. Then, rising, Mrs. Kennedy thanked Brandt for coming and took him to a large window in the White House that overlooked some notable capital landmarks. She said her husband had often stood at that place drawing strength from the history of his country. Brandt and Robert Kennedy then left the room. Robert Kennedy's words of farewell to Brandt were, "He loved Berlin."

CHAPTER IX

The Candidate

In May, 1962, Brandt was elected vice-chairman of his party. Then, after the death of Ollenhauer the SPD elected him chairman, in February, 1964. His battle cry became "Forward to the next election!"

For many reasons, Brandt looked forward to the 1965 elections. The CDU had botched a number of things, including the famous *Der Spiegel* affair. *Der Spiegel*, a German news magazine, had printed a damaging account of the West German army. When the government brutally tried to suppress the magazine by arresting its publisher and charging treason, freedom of the press became a major issue, and a number of important cabinet ministers were forced to resign in disgrace.

The press and his own party criticized Adenauer severely for his role in the affair, so in late 1963, he stepped down as chancellor in favor of his popular Economic Minister Ludwig Erhard.

Meanwhile, everything was looking brighter for the Social Democrats. The opinion polls indicated that an increased number of voters was leaning toward the SPD, especially the young and the city people. The party was also making good use of the many mistakes made by their opponents. It was little wonder that Brandt could tell his party in 1964, "We know today we can win nationally. That has strengthened the self-confidence of our friends."

The opening guns of the election campaign started with Brandt appealing to artists and writers to support his new mass party. When Brandt's opponent, Erhard, fell into an angry tirade over "useless" intellectuals spouting nonsense, two dozen writers immediately organized a committee to support Brandt. The novelists Günter Grass, author of *The Tin Drum,* and Hans Werner Richter wrote slogans and gave speeches, while the playwrights Peter Weiss, author of *Marat/Sade,* and Rolf Hochhuth, author of *The Deputy,* organized advertising campaigns and solicited funds. Unlike the intellectuals of the Weimar Republic days, who did so much to undermine public confidence in the Republic, West Germany's new generation of writers was determined to fight for its new state. "The genius of a writer is in his courage," said Günter Grass. "I believe he must also have the courage to become involved!"

But the star of the SPD campaign was still Brandt. He now seemed more sure of himself, calmer, more the real Willy, and less the German copy of John Kennedy. Even his opponents admitted that he had turned into a formidable campaigner. His relations with the working press were excellent, but he still did not project well over television. His most effective method of campaigning was personal contact, so he again took to the road.

Brandt traveled in a special train equipped with a sleeping car, an office car, a diner, and a freight car, which packed two black Mercedes sedans for use when he stopped. He gave 550 addresses and countless interviews and pounded away at the issues. The German people had not forgotten the horrible lesson of their past history, he said, but they were now looking forward to the future, for they, like all peoples, must have that right.

Brandt's middle son Lars often accompanied his father

The Candidate

on the campaign trips because he wanted to hear the kind of questions that were asked. After the first press conference, Lars seemed satisfied with his father's performance, for he told a reporter, "The questions didn't surprise me and my father had an idea what would be asked and he was ready."

Brandt was ready for the election too, which the polls indicated would be a close one. Yet, after crisscrossing Germany, he felt he was on the edge of victory. His slogan, "Living in Berlin, thinking about Germany—Willy Brandt," seemed to reassure many voters. Everywhere the crowds cheering the young mayor of Berlin grew larger. They loved it when Willy told them, "My party and my team have more in the *Rucksack* [knapsack]."

Four days before the election, Willy was still campaigning hard. At a press conference in Bonn he argued that the voters were tired of the lack of progress on German reunification and the failure to build a more equal society. The election campaign indicated that Germany was ready for a change. Brandt felt that the SPD would win the election.

On the night of September 19, 1965, a tired Willy Brandt rode to the party headquarters in Bonn to watch the returns. By ten o'clock in the evening the television commentators were reporting the victory of the CDU again.

The press corps crowded into Willy's room asking for his reactions to the defeat. A tired Brandt waved his hand, "Let's talk about it tomorrow after we all have had a good night's sleep." There was no hiding his bitter disappointment. To have worked so hard, given so many speeches, come so close, only to lose again was heartbreaking.

"Brandt is finished as a politician," predicted the press. Because he had been twice defeated, they called him the Adlai Stevenson of Germany.

A few days later, Brandt announced that in the best interest of the party he would give up the struggle for power. Bitterly he told the press that the mud slinging and personal attacks had not left him unmarked. He returned to Berlin, where his own party was in revolt. His critics accused him of neglecting his official duties by spending too much time on national politics.

The next half year was one of the hardest Willy spent. Physically drained by the grueling campaign, his health weakened by illness, he was surrounded by critics. Manfully he admitted his election mistake, "Too much image and not enough policy."

The Social Democrats had won 12.7 million votes, about 1.4 million over the previous election. Yet most of them felt that they would have to win at least 40 percent of the vote if they were to become a major party. The SPD had to convince the broad group of middle-class voters that they should forget their traditional dislike of the "socialists" and vote for this new Brandt-led group. In 1965 they had not convinced enough voters.

By June of 1966, the clouds of depression and doubt that hung over Brandt had lifted. Tanned, refreshed, his confidence regained, he told the party, "I did not come here as a bankrupt." He had regained control over his party in Berlin, and at the party conference in Dortmund he was the same old Brandt minus the campaign image. "The year 1965 did not have just one day, September 19, but many days. There wasn't just one decision, but many. Every year brings its chance and what the year 1966 brings lies to a great extent on our own shoulders. Not a thoughtless no of the defeated but a positive yes to Germany's future must be the key to our party's attitude." His party responded to him two days later when 324 of the 326 delegates reelected him chairman of the Social Democrats.

Meanwhile the fortunes of the SPD had risen immeasurably on the national scene as Chancellor Erhard's government stumbled badly. After the 1965 elections, Erhard's ruling coalition government, made up of his own CDU/CSU Party and the small Free Democratic Party, had found itself under fire from all sides. A student revolt in the universities continued to grow, indicating dissatisfaction from the left. At the same time a new ultranationalistic party, the National Democratic Party (NPD), made sensational gains among conservatives in local state elections. The nation seemed to be polarizing between the extreme left and the extreme right.

Erhard also had difficulties with his allies, as sharp differences on foreign policy, economic cooperation, and the future of the European Common Market developed between de Gaulle's France and President Johnson's United States. Erhard tried to play the role of go-between, but ended up getting stung by both sides. At home, for the first time since the war, Germans faced a mild economic recession. Another blow fell to Erhard in July, 1966, when the Social Democrats made considerable gains in the elections in the big state of North Rhine–Westphalia. Erhard's critics, including Adenauer, who had never had much faith in his political abilities, called for his resignation. In October, Erhard's fate was virtually sealed when the Free Democrats announced their intention of leaving the coalition government. A couple of days later the state elections in Hesse finished off the "rubber lion," as Erhard had been nicknamed.

By November 10, the CDU/CSU had agreed on a new chancellor candidate, Dr. Kurt Georg Kiesinger, a polished, smooth, compromise politician who was prime minister of the state of Baden-Württemberg. Unfortunately, Kiesinger had a Nazi past, a fact that did not escape the attention of the world press.

Kiesinger tried to organize another government with the badly divided Free Democrats, but they were not enthusiastic about renewing their partnership in a coalition government with the CDU/CSU. Instead Kiesinger turned to the Social Democrats and sought to bring them into a "Grand Coalition" government.

The leading Socialists were divided on this prospect. Brandt was lukewarm to the idea while most leftist members opposed it. However, an influential group argued that if the SPD would enter such a strong coalition, they might improve their chances with the voters in the next elections. They could prove to the middle-class swing voters that they were competent ministers and able to handle the responsibilities of high office.

Others argued that the polls continued to show a shift to the SPD, and that the best political tactics would be to allow Kiesinger's government to waddle through to the next general election and then defeat him at the polls. At this point, Brandt exercised his leadership by coming out in favor of the Grand Coalition. Germany in those perilous times could not afford a weak government that would drift for three years. It was better to take a chance with Kiesinger than to run the risk of harming Germany.

The Social Democrats entered Kiesinger's new government with Brandt as the vice-chancellor and foreign minister and nine of his fellow socialists as ministers. As Brandt said when he took over the Foreign Office, "No one with a sense of history will find it easy to disregard the Great Coalition of Social Democrats and Christian Democrats, nor the fact that a man of my convictions has become the Foreign Minister of Germany."

It was the first time since the Weimar Republic that Socialists were a part of the government, but many rank-and-file members of the party were still unhappy. They found a spokesman in Günter Grass, the popular novelist, who disliked Kiesinger's Nazi past and who voiced the concern that Brandt had sold out to the Establishment. To make matters worse, in the first year of the coalition the recession deepened and the Social Democrats lost ground in regional elections.

But Brandt was well suited to be foreign minister. His long years of residence abroad, his command of foreign languages, and his obvious interest and liking for foreign affairs combined to make him, in the words of Golo Mann, the historian and son of the famed novelist Thomas Mann, "the best foreign minister the Federal Republic has had."

Brandt began a vigorous reappraisal of West German policy toward Eastern Europe and the German unification question. The broad outline of his *Ostpolitik* (Eastern Policy) was formed during this period. It included an effort to reestablish normal diplomatic relations with the Warsaw Pact countries, the Soviet Union and her Eastern European allies, and the first genuine attempts to talk to the East Germans. The older Cold War doctrines of ignoring East Germany and breaking diplomatic relations with countries that recognized East Germany were abandoned in favor of a more flexible approach.

West Germany established normal relations with Rumania and Yugoslavia and worked toward establishing them with the other Eastern countries, although this policy received a serious setback when the Soviet Union brutally invaded Czechoslovakia in 1968. The Federal Republic's relations with the Third World, the neutral or nonaligned countries, improved also as Brandt became a tireless worker for better understanding for and more trade and economic aid to these lands. Brandt's handling of relations with the NATO countries was sound also. He insisted on maintaining strong ties with the United States, and he was the leading supporter of European unity.

At home the Grand Coalition government found progress somewhat more difficult. Criticism that the Socialists had "sold out" continued unabated. The students became more aggressive, and widespread riots occurred in West Germany in 1967 and in the spring of 1968. Many universities were closed down by radical students protesting the lack of educational reforms and the "sham" of German democracy.

The Socialist German Students' League (SDS), originally set up by the SPD, was a particularly thorny problem. The SDS had always been moderate, but in 1959 it had turned sharply radical left when the Social Democrats accepted the Bad Godesberg program and became moderate. The Social Democrats had to dissociate themselves from the SDS, an act that seemed only to incite the students more toward radicalism. The SPD then helped organize a new Social Democratic University League (SHB), but it too turned radical, much to the embarrassment of the party. However, despite the publicity the radical students received, polls indicated that the great majority of students had no clear political orientation and were hardly leftists.

During the first two years of the Grand Coalition the Social Democrats received a number of electoral reverses in the local and state elections, but in 1969 their political fortunes took a turn for the better. In March, the small Free Democratic Party supported the Socialist candidate for president, Dr. Gustav Heinemann, and he was duly elected, making him the first Social Democrat president since the death of Friedrich Ebert in 1925. Heinemann brought great warmth and informality to the office. Just as important, the support of the Free Democrats in his election indicated that they could be brought into a coalition government with the Socialists.

As the SPD geared for the national elections in the fall of 1969, it was obvious that the Brandt team had an advantage. Willy Brandt was a different person from the young hero of 1960. The lean, hard years of defeat had matured him and strengthened his character. He had proved in defeat that he had the ability to be a true leader. In his years in office as a member of the Grand Coalition government, he had shown outstanding abilities as foreign minister and party leader. He was flexible, determined, and thoughtful in his dealings with his colleagues and subordinates as well as with foreign representatives. He had firmly established himself as a man in the middle of his party. He was someone every side could talk to, argue with, and listen to. His strength lay in carefully hearing out all points of view before finally making up his mind. Willy could not be stampeded into a rash action. He often preferred to wait out developments until he thought they had matured, then to act. The politician had developed into a statesman.

The 1969 elections were a spirited affair featuring the first joint, nationwide television appearance of leaders of the four principal parties. Vital issues separated the parties, including the question of official recognition of East Germany, increased labor participation in management of industry, tax and currency questions, and social policies. On television Brandt's cool reckoning, patience, and appeal to reason offered a sharp contrast to his younger opponents, who were inclined to be impatient and irrational.

Genuine leftists felt that Brandt had "sold out" to the middle class while the extreme right deplored his presence in the government. But the large mass of voters, now increased by a law giving the vote to eighteen-year-olds, showed confidence in Brandt. The strategy of proving that he and his fellow Socialists could be trusted to rule proved successful.

During the difficult campaigning in the last weeks before the election, Brandt made a quick visit to the United Nations in New York. Taking advantage of the opening of the General Assembly, he conferred with eight fellow foreign ministers. When he returned to Bonn, the 150 assembled newsmen expected to find him tired, but instead Brandt was grinning, cracking jokes, and acting as if he were just back from vacation.

He told the newsmen, "I had been a bit down, you know. My vocal chords had gone several times, and I had become depressed by that disgusting routine of campaigning around like a gypsy without being able to do any reasonable work. I had behaved in New York and gone to bed early—ten thirty—and really slept for the first time in weeks. Then I caught some more sleep on the flight back. When I got here, I knew it was just a little bit more to go to the end of the week and the campaign. All at once I felt good."

He had every right to feel good. A few days later, 14 million voters cast their ballots for him. The SPD gained 1.2 million more votes than in 1965 and took 42.7 percent of the total vote. The CDU/CSU captured slightly more votes, but their totals had slipped badly since 1965.

Immediately the parties began negotiations to form a coalition government. On October 28, 1969, Willy Brandt was elected chancellor of West Germany by a mini-coalition of his own Social Democrats and the Free Democrats.

The election climaxed one of the most extraordinary political careers in modern times. By traditional German standards, Willy Brandt had nearly everything against him. Born out of wedlock in a country that had until recently discriminated against illegitimate children, an expatriate in Scandinavia, a Norwegian "officer" after the war, and a member of the Social Democratic Party, a party often denounced as "an enemy of Germany," he had become the fourth chancellor of the Federal Republic of Germany.

"I am," remarked Willy Brandt after his election, "satisfied and thankful for the trust that has been placed in me and a little bit proud that I may serve in this high office." To his close friends he said, "I never knew if I would be chancellor, but I knew that, if I would be, I could do it."

CHAPTER X

Chancellor of Reforms

The election of Willy Brandt as chancellor of the Federal Republic on October 28, 1969, marked a major turning point in the history of Germany. For the first time in nearly forty years a Social Democrat led the nation, and for the first time since the founding of the West German state in 1949 there was a complete changeover of power.

The new coalition government of Brandt's Social Democrats and the Free Democrats enjoyed only a slight majority of twelve seats in the Bundestag. Nevertheless the party immediately outlined a vigorous course of action. In the cabinet the leader of the Free Democrats, Walter Scheel, became vice-chancellor and foreign minister, occupying Brandt's former positions. There were two other Free Democrats in the government. The rest of the cabinet posts were held by the Social Democrats, including key members of the Brandt election team, Karl Schiller, new economics minister, and Helmut Schmidt, defense minister. Käte Strobel became the minister for health, family and youth affairs, indicating Brandt's intention of bringing more women into the highest level of government.

In Brandt's opening address as chancellor, he pledged his government to domestic reforms and continuity in foreign policy. "The policy of domestic reform that our government has adopted," he said, "is meant not only to produce specific social renovation, but also to foster the Federal Republic's internal development as a free, democratic society. The common denominator in our foreign policy can only be to keep the peace." In several press and television interviews shortly after taking office he mentioned his hope that England would be brought into the Common Market. He said the Federal Republic was ready to sign agreements with the Soviet Union and all Eastern European nations renouncing the use or threat of force in international relations.

The world press greeted Brandt's new government with enthusiasm and optimism. The London *Guardian* wrote, "Herr Brandt is a non-conformist and a fighter, and for West Germany this is a change. It comes after 20 years of perfectly respectable but unadventurous democracy." The American magazine *Newsweek* observed, "It is an experiment . . . that Willy Brandt will be conducting as West Germany's new Chancellor, and for both the Christian and Social Democrats, indeed, for the entire nation, it should be a worthwhile one." Even the Russian press had praise for the anti-Nazi and Socialist Brandt.

Brandt moved quickly at home and abroad during the first "Hundred Days" of his new government. A string of new bills were sent to the Bundestag, many study commissions were organized, and much time and effort were put forth to handle the internal problems. Progress was slow as Germany faced growing inflation and rising prices. The German mark (currency) was sharply revalued 9.3 percent upward, which brought some relief among the world's central banks, but it hit German pocketbooks hard. It was now easier to sell foreign goods in Germany, but more expensive for Germans to sell abroad. "Stabilization can hurt," Karl Schiller reminded his countrymen, "stabilization demands sacrifice."

Although Brandt thought of himself as a reform chancellor pledged to get Germany moving again, his greatest successes were to come in the area of foreign affairs. As chancellor he played a leading role in fulfilling his *Ostpolitik* (Eastern Policy) which he had started when he was foreign minister. The *Ostpolitik* was a fresh approach to relations with the Soviet Union, with Germany's eastern neighbors linked to the Soviet Union, and most specifically, with East Germany, in an effort to reduce tensions and prepare for a peaceful European order. As Brandt had said years ago to the Council of Europe, "For centuries, Germany formed a bridge between western and eastern Europe. We intend to rebuild that broken bridge."

Brandt, like de Gaulle in France, had come to the conclusion that the era of the Cold War was drawing to a close and that the era of the détente, the relaxation of tensions between nations, had begun. The Soviet bloc was undergoing massive changes, which opened the doors of opportunity to the West.

The old Ministry of All-German Affairs was now renamed the Ministry of Inter-German Relations. The habit of calling East Germany the "so-called German Democratic Republic" or the "Soviet Zone" was dropped in favor of its correct name, and television weathermen quietly stopped referring to "those parts of old Germany now in Poland and Middle Germany." In short, the old Cold War approach to the German problem was changed as Brandt insisted on starting with the facts. The facts were simple: Germany was divided into two nations, had been for some time, and probably would be for some time in the future. Germans had to realize this.

From his first day in office, Brandt launched the new *Ostpolitik*. He caught friends and foes by surprise. Talks were begun with the Soviet Union, Poland, Czechoslovakia, and East Germany, but Brandt concentrated on Moscow, feeling that once agreements were reached there, the rest of the eastern European states would readily conform. In December Brandt's close adviser, State Secretary Egon Bahr, was sent to Moscow to begin exploratory talks while Brandt proposed a meeting with the heads of the East German state.

On March 19, 1970, for the first time in postwar German history, the chancellor of West Germany set foot on East German soil when, at the old historic town of Erfurt, Willy Brandt met with Willi Stoph, chairman of the Ministerial Council of East Germany. Huge crowds of East Germans turned out to chant, "Willy Brandt! Willy Brandt!" The moving scene of so many East Germans pushing through the barriers to see Willy was watched by millions of television viewers in both parts of Germany. Brandt, fearful that too great a demonstration would cause embarrassment to the East German government and disturb the talks, sought to calm the crowd. He appeared briefly at the window of his hotel and silently raised his hand. A few minutes later he sat down with Willi Stoph and began the talks.

During the first meeting at Erfurt and a second one at Kassel, both sides outlined their positions. Both agreed that "never again would war emanate from German soil." Brandt was not discouraged by the limited accomplishments, and in line with his policy of small steps first, he ordered his State Secretary Bahr to continue the talks. Finally the two German states agreed on an extension of trade and of postal and telephone communications. In addition, an agreement was reached to allow West Berliners visitation privileges behind the Wall.

Relations between the two German states were far from

normal, but Brandt was determined to press on. "I will not be deterred from trying to achieve what I consider to be right and necessary," he told his people, "otherwise I should not have become chancellor."

Basically Brandt argued that there were two German states and one German nation. West Germany could never accept the division of Germany as permanent, even though there were now two separate and distinctly different social systems.

After the Kassel meeting, Brandt proposed a twenty-point program as a basis for negotiations between both Germanys. Most of his proposed points were practical steps concerning mutual relations to establish closer ties between the citizens of the two states. As the former mayor of Berlin, Brandt was particularly sensitive to the many personal family ties that had been broken since the erection of the Berlin Wall.

Brandt's peace offensive caused confusion and uncertainty in East Germany. For years the East Germans had been calling for talks between the two parts of Germany, and now suddenly Brandt was taking them at their word. Quickly the East Germans beat a hurried retreat. They claimed further negotiations between the two Germanys would have to wait until West Germany fully recognized the German Democratic Republic as an independent state.

Brandt was not surprised at their new attitude. "Whatever might be thought about the way things went at Erfurt and Kassel a start has been made. And I am convinced that it won't stay at that," he said. He had other plans to pressure the East Germans into negotiations. The shortest road to East Berlin led through Moscow.

Brandt's talks with Moscow hit a number of snags. The Germans insisted that treaties with the Soviet Union and Poland be tied to an agreement facilitating the smooth flow of transportation between the Federal Republic and Berlin. Moscow insisted that the Federal Republic officially recognize the loss of territories that were now either Russian or Polish. After many grueling rounds of talks, a West German–Soviet treaty renouncing the use of force and accepting the loss of old German territories was signed by Brandt and Soviet Premier Kosygin in Moscow on August 12, 1970.

In a special television address from Moscow to his people, Brandt called the treaty "an important moment in our postwar history. . . . It is a decisive step to improve our relations with the Soviet Union and our Eastern neighbors—a quarter of a century after the catastrophe that demanded unspeakable sacrifices from the peoples, in the East even more than in the West."

Although better access to Berlin was not mentioned in the treaty, Brandt had cleverly tied the treaty to the signing of an agreement over Berlin among the Big Four occupying powers. He insisted that he would not submit the treaty to the West German parliament for formal ratification until a Berlin agreement was reached.

In October, 1970, under pressure from Moscow, the East Germans agreed to reopen talks with the West Germans. In November Foreign Minister Scheel traveled to Warsaw to establish normal relations between Poland and West Germany. By December Brandt was able to travel to Warsaw to sign a Polish–West German treaty.

The most dramatic moment of his visit occurred at the memorial for the murdered Jews of the Warsaw ghetto.

Brandt walked slowly to the memorial and placed a wreath there. Then, instead of simply bowing his head, he suddenly knelt before the memorial. A murmur swept through the crowd.

Later Brandt said, "I thought that it just simply was not enough to bow my head, no, I couldn't just do that." Brandt then spoke of the need to end the quarter century of enmity between the two nations. He expressed the hope that the new treaty would mark the first step on the road to reconciliation.

Brandt's whirlwind *Ostpolitik* during his first year in office as chancellor gained him great international fame. On January 4, 1971, *Time* magazine named him the Man of the Year and called him a great innovator of this time. The magazine praised Brandt and declared: "By becoming the first West German politician willing to accept the full consequences of defeat in World War II, West German Chancellor Willy Brandt moved to shape events rather than react to them and presented a challenge to Communist Europe that has great potential significance for the rest of the world."

Modestly Brandt remarked on hearing about the article, "Actually one should not say too much about it. It's what the English call a challenge."

In his State of the Nation address to the German people on January 28, 1971, Brandt stressed that the government was encouraged to continue along the path of peace and said that he hoped for more personal freedom and more social justice in divided Germany. He noted too that his *Ostpolitik* was complementary to his Western policy of further European cooperation and unification. They belonged together and were the basis for bridging the gap between Eastern and Western Europe.

As for his talks with East Germany, Brandt said, "What is possible among the states in Europe should be possible also between the two states of Germany: The artificial sealing off . . . has brought neither stability nor peace. It has, on the contrary, engendered tensions and crises which have to be overcome in the interests of Europe and Germany."

Through most of 1971, Brandt's foreign policy was involved with the Berlin question. Neither the Soviet treaty nor the Polish treaty was to be ratified until some acceptable agreement on Berlin had been reached by the Soviet Union, England, France, and the United States. To be sure, Brandt continued his talks with other Eastern European states, but there was obvious resistance in East Germany and in some circles of the Russian government over Brandt's *Ostpolitik*. In May, the unexpected resignation of Walter Ulbricht, longtime leader of East Germany, signaled a change in Moscow's thinking. Ulbricht had been staunchly opposed to any concessions to West Germany. A man who had survived many twists and turns of Moscow's policy, he had symbolized the Cold War in East Germany, but now he was unceremoniously dropped, because he was no longer useful.

Throughout the summer Brandt kept his diplomats moving. He encouraged the Western powers to work out an agreement with the Russians on Berlin while he dangled the prospect of rich trade agreements and technological aid before the hungry eyes of Eastern Europeans.

In the Middle East, Africa, and Asia, Brandt's diplomacy was fair and evenhanded. He was able to strengthen Germany's position in these areas by his *Ostpolitik,* because West Germany was no longer subjected to the possibility of international blackmail. Before that, many neutral nations had held a club over West Germany by threatening to recognize East Germany should West Germany not comply with their wishes. That threat was now eliminated.

By September a breakthrough had occurred. The ambassadors of the Four Occupying Powers in Berlin signed an agreement recognizing their joint rights and obligations in Berlin, but also easing access to the city and legalizing the relationship between West Berlin and the Federal Republic. Brandt was satisfied that the new Four-Power Pact over Berlin would ease tensions in that troubled hot spot and also protect the rights of Berliners and West Germans.

Shortly after the Berlin agreement Brandt traveled to the Soviet Union to confer with Leonid Brezhnev, chairman of the Communist Party. The two leaders agreed that a return to normal relations in central Europe was the most important task facing both countries. But Brandt made it very clear that the Soviet and Polish treaties would be ratified only after a satisfactory conclusion to the talks with the East Germans. The Berlin agreement had stipulated that most of the technical details over access rights would have to be worked out by the two Germanys.

Brezhnev spoke of the need for formal diplomatic recognition of East Germany after the Berlin talks, and generally both men agreed that the tension in Europe must relax.

Afterward Brandt commented, "The reactions from London, Paris, and Washington to my talks with Brezhnev are what I had expected. The reactions are based on trust; they state that the German Federal Government's policy

Chancellor of Reforms

of rapprochement with the East is a part of our joint Western policy."

The joint talks between the two German states continued, but progress was slow. In the midst of his diplomatic activities, Brandt received unexpected help from outside. On October 20, 1971, the last day of his first year in office, Willy Brandt was awarded the highest international honor bestowed on a statesman, the Nobel Prize for Peace for 1971.

The award was announced in the middle of a Bundestag debate. Amid the cheers of his colleagues, Brandt thanked all who had contributed to it by saying, "This high award exacts great commitment. I shall do everything to prove myself worthy of this honor in my further work."

The Nobel Prize citation read, in part, "Chancellor Willy Brandt has as chief of the West German Government and in the name of the German people extended his hand for a policy of reconciliation between old enemies. . . . The Nobel Committee sees in this common dedication a basic contribution to the strengthening of the possibilities for a free development, not only in Europe but in the whole world."

It was with some pride that this former refugee to Sweden, this former citizen of Norway traveled back to Oslo and Stockholm in December, 1971, to receive the Nobel Prize. What must have passed through his mind as with trembling hands he accepted this award before the Norwegian parliament? Did he remember those days in 1936 when he had worked so hard to obtain the Nobel Prize for another German, the pacifist Carl von Ossietzky, who was slowly dying in a Nazi concentration camp? Did he recall his long fight for Norway's freedom during the Second World War? Or were his thoughts on his close friends from Scandinavia, many of whom, like the sociologists Alva and Gunnar Myrdal, were in the audience?

His address acknowledging the award dwelt on his country's desire for peace. He spoke of the need to help other countries less fortunate than those in Europe, the need for European unity, and the need to solve Germany's division. He commented on the three other German prize winners of previous years: Gustav Stresemann, who had been foreign minister of Germany in the 1920's and was an architect of Franco-German reconciliation; Ludwig Quidde, the historian and opponent of authoritarianism everywhere; and, of course, Carl von Ossietzky. But most of all Brandt rededicated himself and his government to the search for lasting peace. Only at the dinner speech in Oslo did a personal element creep into his comments when he said, "At that time, as a young man of nineteen, I took with me into exile a vision of a Germany that was noble and just. In spite of all the shame at the crimes that were committed in the misused name of my people, I never lost sight of the prospect of German freedom."

The Nobel Prize and the congratulations it brought from around the world were of tremendous advantage to Brandt in the next few months. Germans of all political persuasion were rightfully proud of their chancellor. Even the East Germans shared in this pride, and shortly thereafter the long-drawn-out negotiations between the two Germanys over the transit agreement for Berlin were successfully concluded. On December 19, 1971, both countries signed the agreement, which implemented the Four-Power agreement on Berlin.

Now that all the preliminary steps had been taken, Brandt submitted the Moscow and Warsaw treaties to the Bundestag for ratification. The crucial moment in his *Ostpolitik* had come; Brandt and his party were in for the political fight of their lives.

Brandt's *Ostpolitik* had won great acclaim abroad, but at home it threatened the existence of his government. His critics argued that he had given too much to the Russians for too little in return. In a country where every fifth person had been a refugee or expellee, there was naturally much resistance to recognizing the loss of older German territories to Poland and Russia. For twenty years many Germans had lived with the illusion that somehow, someway, these territories would be given back to Germany.

Brandt's policies had started with the assumption that Germany had begun a terrible world war and that she would have to pay a price for that action. Part of the price was the loss of territories. But some critics felt that Brandt had dangerously risked changing the *status quo*, or existing situation. His policies might be thought of as an attempt by the Germans to strike a deal with the Russians behind the backs of their Western allies. Opposition to the treaties was deep and widespread, especially in the Christian Democratic Party and its sister party, the Christian Socialists (CDU/CSU). There were even some doubts among Brandt's governing coalition of Social Democrats and Free Democrats.

In October, 1969, when Brandt had formed his coalition government, his majority in the Bundestag was only a slim twelve votes. During the course of the next three years six members of the governing coalition went over to the CDU/CSU opposition, robbing the government of their precarious majority. By the time the Bundestag started debating the ratification of the Moscow and Warsaw treaties, a stalemate existed there with both the government and the opposition holding the same number of votes.

One way out of this situation was for Chancellor Brandt to call for and intentionally lose a vote of confidence in the Bundestag, thus forcing a general election before it was normally due. Brandt rejected this approach, for he preferred to push through the ratification of the treaties and rule the nation until the next scheduled election in the fall of 1973.

His desire was blocked, however, when Rainer Barzel, the leader of the Christian Democrats, decided to challenge the government by calling for a no-confidence vote. Since opinion polls had indicated that a majority of citizens supported Brandt's *Ostpolitik,* Barzel claimed the vote was based on the domestic policies of Brandt. But it was clear to all that the principal differences were over Brandt's foreign policy.

On April 27, 1972, for the first time in West Germany's history, a motion of no-confidence was submitted to the Bundestag. Tensely the citizens of the entire nation dropped whatever they were doing and watched the television as the historical vote was cast. With an emotion-charged voice, the president of the Bundestag announced the results: three abstentions and 247 votes for the motion. The vote of no-confidence had failed by *one* vote; Brandt's government was saved.

Socialist deputies wildly threw their arms around one another, and cheers went up in many German cities as millions breathed sighs of relief. A grave parliamentary crisis had been overcome.

Incidentally, it was clear that at least one CDU or CSU

member must not have voted for Barzel, and there were many dark rumors about huge bribes being paid to hold or buy votes.

After withstanding the no-confidence vote, Brandt's government moved ahead. On May 17, 1972, the Moscow and Warsaw treaties were approved by the Bundestag although the coalition did not have an absolute majority. The CDU/CSU was split on the issue, and after a dramatic series of discussions decided to abstain from voting as a party. The vote was 248 for the treaties, 10 against, and 238 abstentions.

Brandt's last step in his *Ostpolitik* now followed. The two German states began talks that finally led, in December, 1972, to their signing a Basic Treaty, which defined the future basis of their relations. Each part of Germany recognized the territorial integrity and sovereignty of the other, and both renounced the use of force against one another. In effect, the two Germanys were recognizing legally what both had known for twenty years—that Germany was two very different states.

The Basic Treaty paved the way for formal diplomatic recognition of East Germany by the Western allies and the entrance of both Germanys into the United Nations in 1973. West Germany, still clinging to Brandt's doctrine of "two states in one nation," did not formally recognize East Germany, but rather exchanged diplomatic missions, a step slightly below formal diplomatic acceptance.

In commenting on this treaty, Brandt told reporters on November 9, "The Basic Treaty . . . opens the way to the normalization that is now possible. . . . It alters nothing in the basic difference existing with the German Democratic Republic."

But Brandt was hopeful that for the first time since the

division of the country a way had been found of "beginning to bridge the resultant chasm." The press labeled it a promissory note for the future, but at least it marked a change in the way relations between the two countries were conducted. At the practical level the treaty allowed all Germans the same rights of citizenship in both parts of Germany, and it eased communications and travel between them. To this extent, as Brandt remarked, the Cold War was over.

The crisis in the coalition government because of the Moscow and Warsaw treaties was finally solved by Brandt on June 24, 1972. He called for new elections one year before they were normally scheduled. To avoid a conflict in the midst of the Olympic Games in Munich, they were scheduled for November 19.

Public opinion polls in the spring and summer continued to show that Brandt had a wide majority over his CDU rival Rainer Barzel. Even the sensational resignation of his longtime adviser and top minister Karl Schiller on July 7 did not seriously cut into his popularity. Throughout the late summer and early fall Brandt maintained his lead, and the Social Democrats went into the elections confident of victory. Their slogans emphasized the need for keeping Willy Brandt on the job. His international fame, his *Ostpolitik,* and his pledges of reform at home were the major offensive weapons of the Socialists. The smaller Free Democrats (FDP) campaigned with the same assurance. They were willing and eager to remain in the government with Brandt's party.

The campaign of 1972 was as hard as the previous ones for Brandt, with its long hours of travel, the speech-making, and the countless appearances before the press and the television cameras. The demands of his work did not prevent Brandt from devoting his full energy to the elections. He hired a train and whistle-stopped throughout Germany, as eager a politician seeking votes as he had been as a young man in 1959. Friends such as the novelist Günter Grass helped by renting campers so he could travel to remote places and give speeches. Movie stars, soccer players, TV personalities, writers, and musicians signed supportive pledges for him, but the lion's share of the campaign was still done by Brandt. Although his rival, Barzel, limited himself to three speeches a day, Brandt spoke four, five, and six times a day. He seemed to be everywhere; his party flooded the country with full-color campaign posters of a bulldog face—smiling Willy Brandt. *"Willy muss Kanzler bleiben"* ("Willy must remain Chancellor") was the favorite slogan of his campaign. The crowds seemed to sense that Willy was more popular than the party he led.

Brandt was vulnerable on a number of issues. Inflation was roaring along at a 6.2 percent per year rate, and many felt that the government had not done enough to solve the staggering problems of pollution, traffic, and long-overdue educational reforms. His foreign policy was attacked by the CDU, but since most Germans seemed to be in favor of it, the CDU concentrated instead on the spiraling cost of living and on law and order as the issues that would get votes.

The results of the November 19 election were highly gratifying for Brandt. The SPD scored a decisive victory, gaining 46.2 percent of the vote and electing 230 deputies to the Bundestag, while their opponents, the CDU/CSU, received 44.8 percent and 224 seats. The Free Democrats increased their vote to 8.4 percent, with 42 seats, which meant that the coalition government of Brandt and Scheel now enjoyed a 48-seat majority. For the first time since the founding of the Federal Republic of Germany twenty-three years before, the Social Democrats were the largest party in the Bundestag.

Reaction from the world press was enthusiastic. *"Wunderbar* Willy Back in Triumph!" screamed the headlines of the London *Daily Mirror,* while the Baltimore *Sun* commented that the Germans could be proud of their country. Numerous papers called Brandt the "strong man in Europe," and nearly all of them saw in his victory further proof of a growing German political maturity and a vote of confidence for Brandt's policies of ending the Cold War. In addition, the foreign press was as elated as was Brandt himself by the poor showing of extremist parties. The National Democratic Party (NPD) and the Communist Party (DKP) combined had received less than 1 percent of the total vote.

Brandt's glittering election victory of 1972 did not blind him to the important work that now had to be done. He knew that his domestic policy since 1969 had been less than he and his voters had hoped for. Most of his time since he became chancellor had been devoted to foreign affairs. But his Official Policy Statement (a State of the Union address) delivered to the newly elected Bundestag on January 18, 1973, indicated that domestic problems would now receive most of his attention.

While he was proud that his government could build upon what had been achieved, Brandt's policy statement struck a new theme for his next four years in office.

"Everyday is not a bad word: it has a flavor of our daily bread about it; it has to do with the quality of life, is the aim of our work." While noting the vast improvement in the standard of living for his citizens, Brandt cautioned that "yet more production does not automatically mean more freedom for the individual. Quality of life is more than the standard of living. It is the enrichment of our life over and beyond income and consumption. It presupposes a new understanding of the common good. It increasingly depends on how much of the spirit of good-neighborliness exists among us and on what community facilities are doing for the common good."

Brandt then proceeded to outline his proposed reforms. The budget and rising prices had to be checked and stabilized. Tax structures had to be reformed to allow the average citizen to share in the productive output of major companies. This meant also the right of workers to participate in the management of industry. The pollution of German rivers and streams had to be quickly controlled because, as Brandt noted, "We cannot live at the expense of nature." In a country with such a high density of population (661 persons per square mile, compared to 58.9 persons in the United States), the problem of pollution and proper land utilization was more than just an academic one; it was of immediate vital concern.

The new policy was also aimed at vast improvements in education. Despite its great wealth, the Federal Republic had spent less on education than any industrial nation. Brandt pledged his government to build more schools and to open the restricted educational system so that more students from the lower socioeconomic groups could have access to higher education. At the same time, the vocational schools would be upgraded to the standards of traditional forms of education. The universities were especially singled out for reform. Periods of study were to be shortened, restrictions of the total number of students admitted were to be gradually abolished, and the internal governing of the universities was to be reformed. But Brandt warned, "Centers of teaching and research must not be transformed into political battlegrounds. Knowledge and truth cannot be decided by majority."

Brandt's ambitious program of government was barely launched when he was sharply criticized for not going far enough. His critics were new members of his own Social Democratic Party. Under Brandt's leadership, the party had had extraordinary success in gaining new members, and most of them were not workers, but young people, especially college and high school students, many of whom were more Marxist-oriented than Brandt.

At the party convention in April, 1973, the new members tried to steer the party to the left. Brandt fought what he termed a prefabricated ideology. In a blunt, forthright speech he criticized the "fanatics, idealists, and opponents of the system" who used a "plethora of high-falutin foreign words" and who manifested such a "disgraceful spirit of contempt for the individual." Brandt reminded them that tolerance started with one's choice of words, and that he much preferred "straightforward German" to the sociological or political-science jargon used by the left.

Brandt placed himself squarely in the middle of his party, accepting the basic Bad Godesberg program of 1959 as his guideline. As always, his speech sounded a keynote of integration rather than provocation, and the conference

Chancellor of Reforms

responded by reelecting him chairman of the party with a resounding 404 votes out of a possible 435.

The extent of Brandt's domestic reforms will be seen in the next few years. West Germany, like other industrial nations, faces the serious problems of inflation, youth unrest, urban congestion, lawlessness, and pollution. The West German government possesses some advantages, however. It has a solid majority in the parliament, full employment, a sound economy, and recognized leadership in Willy Brandt.

CHAPTER XI

Moments for Privacy

What does a look at Willy Brandt, the man, reveal?

Brandt is five feet ten and a half inches tall and weighs two hundred pounds, but he reduces that slightly each year at Bad Kreuth, a health resort. He has high, broad cheekbones, steep eyebrows, narrow blue-gray eyes, a high forehead and a strong jaw, and a broad, ruggedly handsome, etched face. His sparse salt-and-pepper hair is set off by an unruly forelock, which Rut describes thus: "It has the same relationship to the rest of his hair as Berlin has to the Federal Republic." Add to this his square, huskily built body, the exactness of his walk, and his conventional gray or dark-blue tailor-made clothes, and the result is an elegant appearance. In 1967, for example, the German tie institute voted him "tie wearer of the year," and he has been ranked among Germany's best-dressed political figures.

In his off hours, Brandt prefers casual sport shirts, jerseys, turtleneck sweaters, and Bavarian-style shooting jackets, but regardless of his dress, he is always comfortable in what he does. He hates diplomatic pomp, although he accepts the occasional necessity of appearing in evening dress with ribbons and decorations over the chest, but he is just as ready to drink a beer with workers at a corner bar.

Brandt has never lost his ability to speak the language of the ordinary citizen. He is the same whether he is speaking to journalists or to his sons or to his chauffeur. Brandt's official biographer wrote, "If there is a formula for the success of citizen Brandt, it is this: He is indeed always a man of the people—the German and the Scandinavian—all in all, the European people."

Brandt is simple, direct, and unassuming, and his preferences, whether in friendships, hobbies, food, or conversation are those of the people. "Old ties of friendship are stronger than new," he confesses. "When I meet people from the old days, I try to find more time for them than I can spare for new friends. Meetings on the frontier —as for example those I frequently had in Denmark with political friends from North Germany—always made a powerful impact on me."

Brandt's hobbies, too, are those of a man who chooses simplicity to complexity. He enjoys watching TV specials, fishing, walking, swimming, and, occasionally, skiing, but most especially reading. Brandt reads avidly on his free weekends, on holidays, and in bed. He prefers politics and history, especially modern history, biographies, technical books, and semidocumentary novels. He says: "Besides my bed and near my desk there are the books I would like to read, and then keep stored away. I only read modern literature during vacations. I read Günter Grass Saturday night and Sunday morning." For the mountains of official material he must read daily, Brandt uses a speed-reading technique.

Music, not a part of young Brandt's life, became important to him only as an adult. "I grew up in an era when . . . there existed not only labor sports, but also labor stamp collectors and labor mandolin players. But I didn't really come into contact with music until the year 1936 in Berlin, when I lived there illegally for half a year. I was, after all, twenty-two years old. I went quite regularly to the Philharmonic concerts. There, a new world opened up for me." Among Brandt's favorite composers are Beethoven, Bach, and Grieg. But he says, "When I was little, I liked military music, and I played in a mandolin orchestra. That was a part of the labor movement. In recent years I have found to my own surprise that I also like modern composers. I have listened to some of their works and think I understand them."

When asked about his favorite food, Brandt listed smoked meat and spring cabbage, a Norwegian dish called Farikal (stewed lamb and cabbage), boiled beef and horseradish sauce, lentil soup, potato pancakes, and lobster. He drinks Moselle wine, Campari and soda, port, or Coca-Cola with a dash of brandy; on warm summer days he prefers beer. He no longer chain-smokes cigarettes but prefers cigarillos.

Although Brandt had been a hard-working politician for years, the role of the chancellor demanded renewed dedication. To the surprise of many of his aides and friends, he shouldered the new responsibility easily. A man who, by his own admission, starts the day slowly, he rises at 7:00 A.M. and reads the morning papers and *Nachrichtenspiegel,* a news sheet compiled by the German News Agency and delivered to him by courier. On the way to his offices in the Palais Schaumburg he studies papers and makes preliminary notes. The Mercedes 300 SE bearing the chancellor's license plate, "0-2," arrives in time for him to study the most important telegrams from German ambassadors abroad. Then he holds a morning conference, or *Lage,* usually at 8:30 A.M. in the small cabinet room. Nicknamed "morning prayers," this conference is the one where policy is planned and decisions are made, and it is attended by Brandt's closest associates in the chancellory. The remainder of his day is taken by appointments.

Brandt's staff members have described him thus: "In the morning he's grumpy, after lunch alert, and in the evening thoroughly charming."

Brandt usually gets home in the early evening, a time when he is spared all but the most prestigious diplomatic social affairs. At home he enjoys his family at dinner, discusses family matters, or even watches television. Then, until bedtime, around 11:00 P.M., he reads or works in his study, where he takes notes with a heavy, black, felt-tipped pen.

Even though Brandt has had many changes in his political life, his personal role as husband and father is secure. In addition, Rut, his wife, is important to his career. Rut has never forgotten her wartime life in Norway, and it has made her more aware of the turmoil in Germany since the war. An example of this is an experience she had when the Brandts were living in Berlin before the Wall was built. They did not live far from the zonal borders, and often East Germans appeared in the neighborhood to sell something or to ask for help. In those years they were conspicuous by their worn-out clothing. One day some transport workers chased an East German away from the Brandts' door, telling him that "Russians" had no business being there. Bewildered, Rut asked if things had gone so far in Germany that West Germans now regarded East Germans as foreigners.

Such memories have heightened Rut's appreciation of the rebirth of German society and her understanding of her own role as chancellor's wife. In 1959, when Brandt had to travel extensively, visiting many capitals, touring the United States, and flying half around the world, Rut accompanied him. Brandt later wrote, "She was—and not only on these travels—an inestimable help to me. Her naturalness, simplicity, and charm made her an excellent ambassador of Berlin. To me she has always been a great support in the haste and turmoil of the political life."

"My best friend is my wife," expresses Brandt's appreciation for Rut's aid on the long way up the political ladder and her continuing help through the countless incriminating political campaigns waged against Brandt by his opponents. Brandt's colleagues, too, recognize the great asset he has in a wife like Rut, who is independent yet supporting. One of Rut's many admirers described her as "that tangy unpretentious Scandinavian simplicity is what lends this attractive woman her special charm." In public she moves with tact, self-assurance, and subtlety. She is a perfect hostess and chancellor's wife.

Although Rut's career as a journalist in the military mission in Berlin was important to her, her marriage, home, and family now come first. Brandt continues to be grateful to her for this choice. Their three sons, all born in Berlin, occupy an important place in both their lives. Peter was born in 1948, during the blockade, the second son Lars was born in early summer 1951. Matthias, the third son, did not come along until 1961.

An independent woman, Rut encourages her sons to live their own lives too. As for herself, she asserts, "I refuse to allow myself to be placed in a cage." One manifestation of her independence came when she refused to move to the official chancellor's residence on the grounds of the elegant Palais Schaumburg, but preferred a more normal family life in their comfortable fourteen-room house in Bonn's residential section, Venusberg, where they lived when Brandt was foreign minister. Rut can shop unobserved in the neighborhood, and her sons, when they are home, can don the hippie clothing they prefer and not be noticed.

Avoiding the press, however, is difficult. The boys lead active, open lives, but as sons of the chancellor, they know the press will make every use of an activity that seems unusual. For example, at sixteen, Peter openly expressed his feelings about the United States' military intervention in Vietnam at a youth-club conference. The incident was used by the press to question Willy Brandt's fitness as a leader.

On a later occasion, when the film *Cat and Mouse*, based on Günter Grass's novel, was made, Brandt's two older sons, Lars, fifteen, and Peter, eighteen, played the same student at two different ages. The story is about a schoolboy who has an Adam's apple larger than normal, and he tries to compensate for his inferiority complex by wearing a Knight's Cross, a coveted medal, which he has stolen from a German naval officer. After being expelled from school he joins the German army, where he is eventually decorated with the Knight's Cross.

Brandt was criticized for letting his sons participate in a dance scene in the movie during which Lars donned bathing trunks and wore the cross around his neck and at his waist. In one letter the writer said the film "shows how the Brandt family regards the military profession and military honor," and then, after noting that Brandt was then foreign minister, concluded, "Poor Germany."

Brandt's attitude toward the press coverage of his sons and the subsequent criticism he sometimes receives is shown in a comment he once made. When Peter was twenty-two and Lars nineteen, they copied the mod styles and anti-Establishment posture of the rest of West Germany's youth. In addition, when Peter was a student at West Berlin's Free University, he was arrested twice for participating in demonstrations and was fined $40 and $68. Asked about these escapades, Brandt shrugged his shoulders and said, "Anyone who has not been a radical before he is twenty will never make a good Social Democrat."

Now that Brandt is chancellor, father and sons have declared a truce, and they do not discuss one another's politics in public. But Brandt has always openly discussed politics with his sons at home, even though the discussions never occurred as often as Brandt would have liked. "When I was elected mayor," he wrote, "I promised myself that I would spend at least one hour every day with my family. I could not keep this promise very often. When I reached our little house in the suburbs where we continue to live after my election, it is usually late in the evening, my boys are already in bed. Lunch or dinner together we can have only on Sunday, but many a Sunday I am out of town on official business.

"It is hard for me, not being able to devote myself to Peter and Lars and Matthias as much as I would like. Boys of their age . . . need the guidance of their father. I only hope that soon there will be more peaceful times which will grant me a more normal life. Fortunately, both my wife and the boys are intelligent enough to accept the inevitable, though the boys have asked quite often why their father could not find a decent job so that he could be at home at a definite hour like all other fathers."

When Brandt was asked about his resolution to reserve an hour each day for his family, he said, "I guess struggling young politicians shouldn't make so many resolutions if they hope to get anywhere."

Although Brandt sometimes suffers the barbs of the press because of his sons, he realizes that they are typical of the youth of West Germany. In a talk with the press, Brandt referred to a protest meeting called in Berlin. "If I know my son Peter," he sighed, only half joking, "he will be there."

This attitude of easy acceptance may be the key to the great rapport Brandt has with young people. He gets along with them much better than do other German politicians. In a recent interview Brandt attributed his success to his own rebellious youth. At one time, he said, he lived in direct opposition to the majority of the citizens. He had the courage and will to resist the weak, ill-advised politics of the Weimar period, and he was only nineteen when he fled Germany. Certainly his own "rebellious youth" gives him greater awareness of the problems and aspirations of contemporary youth.

"It never enters my head to condemn the younger generation. On the contrary," he told the Bundestag in 1968, "I understand why young people become baffled by the contradictions between old practices and new possibilities." On another occasion he commented, "We need the challenge of the younger generation, otherwise we shall get into a rut."

Brandt refused to exert his paternal authority over his politically radical son Peter. "You can't pay less respect to the arguments and convictions of a son simply because he happens to be young," he said. Besides, as many fathers know, "Sons are often more difficult to convince than politicians."

Certainly, a part of Brandt's appeal to the young is because he himself is still a relatively young man. Brandt's appointment as chancellor at fifty-six years of age in 1969 came at a time when barriers of age, social position, and seniority as necessary for success in Germany were being broken down. Both the head of West Germany's largest shipyard and the president of West Berlin's Free University were in their thirties. Brandt's age, then, became an asset, for it was a symbol of the enthusiastic, politically involved, aware youth of West Germany.

More than willing to let youth vent its opinion, Brandt felt that young people should live active political lives. He argued that only recently the party directorate had agreed to accept sixteen-year-olds upon his recommendation. Brandt felt that if they are going to vote in elections at eighteen, they should be able to participate in party activities at sixteen.

"I sincerely believe," he wrote, "that in this country we wait too long before men and women can assume really important political responsibilities. The increased experience that they contribute when they are past fifty is purchased with a goodly share (I don't exactly want to call it resignation) of compromise with all possible difficulties. For myself, I don't think of it as resignation. But herein lies part of our conflict with the younger generation. They feel that the old and middle aged might already have made so many compromises with their equals, with life and with the world, that they can no longer confront the new tasks of today without preconceptions."

In this respect, Brandt is more easily identified with youth than with age. Nevertheless, a typical session over which he presides may end without a vote even though Brandt may hold a strong opinion on the matter. He is willing to "let things develop." He is patient enough to let a decision mature of itself until it begins to give imperceptible little nudges in his direction. Sometimes the decision comes only after a very long time, but Brandt is willing to wait.

On the other hand, Brandt believes in the art of skillful persuasion, also. He knows how to manipulate people. One critic wrote, "He sends a trusted associate in to get the lay of the land, by stimulating discussion of certain issues. Then the associate causes the discussion to be dropped, as though for the time being it isn't so important; then Brandt sends a second emissary into battle, who restimulates the discussion; it develops . . . and then he himself moves in bringing it to fruition. That indicates mastery and cool calculation."

One of Brandt's friends remarked admiringly that he was much more cunning than many people realized. Brandt uses his power with great care, not because of weakness or fear to be strong willed, but because he knows that patience and persuasion are the ways to build longer-lasting leadership. This realization has come only through the great experience Brandt has had in the political ring since he was a young blue-shirted worker in the Socialist Labor Party.

Brandt's attitude toward the sustained power he has tried to build was revealed during an interview when the chancellor said, "In the early fifties, before I became mayor of Berlin, Rut looked at me in horror when I said I wanted power. She considered this something quite evil and had a hard time accepting it. Now she has long understood what I really meant. One seeks influence in a democratic state in order to accomplish something reasonable. That alone counts."

Then Brandt was asked what the root of his power was.

Brandt is too young to project a father image as Adenauer did. He does not have the temperament for dictatorial decisions. Therefore, he answered the question this way: "I try to listen, not only to the young, but also to my associates in the party. I also try to consider differing opinions and finally to find a common denominator of convictions. . . . And I believe that my party basically realizes that I don't want to steamroller anybody. On the other hand, when I feel that a cause is just, I support it wholeheartedly. I have been forced to do that, thank God, only on occasion. There were situations in which I later realized I had overstepped my limits. But my relationship of trust with my party didn't suffer from it. . . . I believe the party feels I treat it fairly."

Brandt's strength of character has been tested many times: by the opposition who degraded him in smear campaigns, by the trials of his work in Berlin, by the failures he experienced in reaching for the chancellorship, and by the Soviets and their constantly changing tactics. One author writes, "There are probably politicians who write more brilliantly—more exciting leaders than he—quicker to catch fire and inspire others. But there is no one who embodies quiet strength more perfectly than he."

Although Brandt has long been considered a maverick because of his political affiliation and his personal heritage, the character assassinations and whispering campaigns never made him bitter or mean. He was able to stand up in the face of the cruel criticism and defend himself openly and objectively when it was necessary. Brandt's work as mayor of Berlin is testimony to his strength. One of Brandt's friends said, "Being mayor of Berlin is a little like operating a meat grinder from the inside." With surety and dispatch Brandt oversaw Berlin through some of its most critical times.

Perhaps the most crucial test of Brandt's strength came in his dealings with the Soviets. When Khrushchev issued his Berlin ultimatum, it was Brandt who, without his party's support, rejected the ultimatum as unacceptable, living up to his reputation for being able to think coolly in moments of crisis under Soviet pressure. Brandt continues to be open to lines of communication with the Soviets, and he is willing to talk to all visitors who come through Berlin from the east.

A young companion of Brandt once said, "He is the biggest catcher we've got. He can take more punishment than anyone." This was especially true after Brandt's defeats as chancellor. He withdrew after the campaigns and went into a deep personal decline. Bouts with heavy drinking earned him the nickname "*Weinbrandt* Willy" (Brandy Willy). A combination of the guidance of close friends and the toughness of his own character brought him through, and he emerged a stronger, more dynamic man.

The international press is as kind to Brandt as German writers, who consider him a favorite and friendly subject. One writer describes Brandt this way, "He is free of pretensions and greedy ambitions; one who has learned to keep his eye on the ball; not to let personal problems distract him from the realities—in short, one who no longer takes himself quite so seriously."

When one of his friends asked him what the real motivation was behind his actions, he gave the remarkable answer: "I want to help." A correspondent in a German weekly wrote, "After his visit to President Kennedy, Washington lies at Willy Brandt's feet, something that does not happen to a politician every day."

Novelist Erich Maria Remarque wrote in a letter to Brandt when he was newly appointed foreign minister, "To Germany's good fortune, you have accepted your new office. By doing so you have given everyone who really cares for Germany a feeling of security. And that security no one but you was able to provide. We are grateful and happy you have done so."

When Brandt was elected chancellor the Elbe, Germany, Union of Ships' Pilots sent him this telegram: AS THE NEW PILOT OF OUR SHIP OF STATE WF WISH YOU GOD SPEED AND A STEADY FOOT OF WATER BENEATH YOUR KEEL. *Christ und Welt,* a Stuttgart weekly, stated, "His popularity can easily compare with the Volkswagen's." Charles de Gaulle said, "Willy Brandt is a sincere and honest man," and the Washington *News* called him "one of postwar Europe's most dynamic and exciting men."

In a number of polls conducted in Eastern Europe, Brandt ranked as the most popular foreign personality by a wide margin. In world opinion polls he has consistently been named one of the ten most admired men in the world today.

Of himself, Brandt says, "It is hard to judge oneself. Anyway, I'm no rhinoceros."

But when judging Germany, Brandt is more specific and more objective. An interviewer asked, "What binds you to Germany and to the Germans, that you return, change occupational direction, and personal life?" He answered, "I always considered Hitler a traitor to the nation. Not just because of the rubble he left behind. Perhaps I would not always have said it like this. What person knows for

Moments for Privacy

certain what he was thinking thirty years ago? To me, Nazism was not only treason to the nation, but also treason to Europe. What binds me is the language, the culture; also the potential of this nation, whose defeat was more severe than that of others, partially through its own fault —but which, therefore, has more possibility of doing something for itself and for others, if it so desires."

Brandt does not consider himself a judge of history, but rather a witness. That is why he can say, with authority, that he has never lost his respect for the German people. The people, on their side, have never lost their respect for Willy Brandt.

CHAPTER XII

A Man for All Europe

Willy Brandt is often referred to as a new European, a man who sees all Europe as his homeland. Brandt lived for many years in Norway and Sweden, and he speaks Norwegian, Swedish, Spanish, French, and English. He is married to a Norwegian. He spends his vacations abroad and seems at home everywhere. He thinks nothing of skiing in the French Alps, swimming on Spain's Costa Brava, or camping on Yugoslavia's Adriatic Coast. These experiences have made him more cosmopolitan than the average European politician. With the fast automobile, the superhighway, and television, Europe has become a single land to Brandt, as it has for most of the Europeans who have grown up since World War II. It is only natural then that Brandt's attitude toward a new, united Europe is different and more comfortable than that of previous generations.

His concept of a united Europe is based on two ideas: economic-political progress and inclusion of the East. Political unity, he feels, is not a dream of idealists but a goal within the sight of this generation. Brandt's view of Europe includes Eastern Europe and the Soviet Union. To use the much-quoted expression of General de Gaulle, Brandt's Europe stretches "from the Atlantic to the Urals." Of course, he is realistic enough to know that this new Europe will not happen overnight, that the Soviet bloc will not dissolve quickly, and that Europeans will not soon give up their national sovereignty and organize into a United States of Europe. But Brandt is convinced that in the meantime many practical steps must be taken to promote this unity because it will not evolve alone.

The Europe that is now growing was born in the ashes of World War II. Never had there been such destruction. Europeans felt that their thousand-year civilization was close to total ruin in 1945. Their colonies gone, their cities in rubble, their wealth spent, their young dead, their political power in the hands of Europe's offspring, America and Russia, the Europeans realized that their only hope lay in burying their own terrible hatreds and in building a Europe that was united and peaceful. As Brandt remarked recently on his first official visit to Israel, "Mankind is lost without courage to start again."

In 1948, the Americans offered the Marshall Plan to help the Europeans economically, but it was Europeans like Jean Monnet, the French planner, and Robert Schuman, the French foreign minister, who designed the first successful practical plans for uniting Europe by pooling the coal and steel industries of Western Germany, France, Italy, the Netherlands, Belgium, and Luxembourg.

By 1957 these six countries had extended their economic cooperation into a customs union called the European Economic Community, or Common Market. Economic cooperation, it was hoped, would encourage political cooperation and, possibly, political unity. This first generation of postwar European leaders, including Konrad Adenauer of Germany, did much to tie the New Europe together economically. The next generation of leaders, such as Brandt, feel that there is much more to be done politically.

One of Brandt's first tasks as foreign minister and later as chancellor was to broaden the Common Market. Brandt made it very clear in his first official announcement as chancellor in October, 1969, that his government was pledged to include countries that sought access to the Common Market, and at a summit conference at The Hague, Netherlands, in December, 1969, the original six Common Market countries agreed to open negotiations with England, Denmark, Norway, and Ireland. After three years of talks these four countries were admitted into the Common Market on January 22, 1972.

"The integration of Western Europe has taken a big step forward," Brandt told his countrymen. "That the Common Market is being broadened is in itself very important. During this decade it is to become an economic and monetary union, and simultaneously the aim will be to strengthen political cooperation. The Community of the Ten must look abroad. It will be judged not the least by its ability to contribute to world peace. To make this contribution means first a good partnership with the United States; it means, secondly, better cooperation with Eastern neighbors; thirdly, it means helping to develop Asia, Africa and Latin America." He added, "I believe that to a major extent Western Europe can become a leading economic and socially conscious region."

The new Europe will be the most progressive region socially in the world. As Brandt told his fellow Europeans on April 13, 1972, "Our task will now be to see to it that social progress in the broad sense of the term is not considered merely as an appendage of economic growth. It must become instead a cornerstone upon which the future interior development of the Community in all its aspects will be built."

But how, it might be asked, is this new Europe to be built, given the mistrust between East and West and the long history of nationalistic pride among all Europeans?

Brandt's answer would be that only through the slow, small steps of improving relations between nations can this be accomplished. International tensions have to be reduced, disarmament agreements made, economic and cultural contacts strengthened, and suspicions and fears eliminated before much progress can be expected.

In line with this thinking, the first step has already been taken; Brandt's government was quick to approve in 1969 the Non-Proliferation of Atomic Weapons Treaty whereby West Germany pledged again not to construct atomic weapons, even though most experts agree that she is capable of doing so. A second small step was taken in Brandt's *Ostpolitik*, when Germany agreed to respect the present borders of her Eastern neighbors. Individually the signing of one treaty or the protecting of a country is not significant, but collectively they develop an atmosphere of trust and cooperation.

The strengthening of cultural ties between peoples of different backgrounds and political systems is especially important to Brandt. Too often the press gives the impression that cultural-exchange programs are unimportant. But to Brandt, the exchange of students, competition among athletes, and the free flow of tourists between nations are highly desirable ways to build mutual trust and confidence. National leaders can sign treaties, pledge words, and make formal declarations of peace, but only when individuals from different countries work and play together will the age-long hatreds of Europeans disappear.

Brandt's encouragement of personal relationships already worked between France and Germany. Ever since

World War II these two traditional enemies have built close people-to-people connections that have largely overcome the hostility. Thousands of students and young apprentices from industry, artists, performers, and athletes have studied and worked in each other's countries every year. Nearly every major German town has a "French House," where French newspapers, books, and products can be seen or bought. The larger German and French towns exchange information and compare common problems and solutions.

In 1963, this cooperation between France and Germany was capped by a treaty that bound both national governments to close and frequent coordination of their policies. In their own quiet way, the German-French programs have been the success story of postwar Europe.

There is, however, a great difference between exchanging students and full political unity. Brandt knows that, which explains why he has led moves to strengthen the Common Market; he wanted to see integration of Western Europe.

The Common Market lands plan to introduce a common form of money by 1980, common units of measurement, common road and tourist signs, and a closer exchange of television. Already the Common Market countries allow the free flow of goods and labor across their frontiers, and it is hoped that once they have a common currency, they will need common banking, taxation, and spending policies. This would mean, of course, that the very heart of governmental activities, the powers to tax and spend, would soon have to be entrusted to the international community.

Economic unity would be followed by political unity, which would recognize individual differences between the

European peoples but build on their obvious need to cooperate with each other. To Brandt and his fellow new Europeans, a divided and fragmented Europe is no match for the power and influence of such continent-wide nations as the United States and Russia. Only in unity can Europe maintain itself and play the role its rich history and traditions entitle it to play in the world.

Naturally there have been and will be many setbacks before European unity is achieved. After Norway was admitted to the Common Market, the Norwegians held a national vote on the issue, and the voters turned it down. The Common Market countries have, at times, been on the verge of breaking apart in their disputes over a common agricultural policy, but somehow they have managed to stick together. Compromises were made, concessions granted, and the Common Market continued.

A good rule for the makers of a united Europe might be one Brandt applied to his first year in office as chancellor. He said he did not wish "to apply the yardstick of the pessimist, but to have the courage of the self-controlled optimist." The vision of a united Europe takes optimism, but hard work too.

What of the Soviet Union in the united Europe? Brandt feels that most of Eastern Europe is culturally tied to the West. Besides, the East is now in need of the technological and financial help that only the West can give. The Soviet Union and her Eastern European allies will be drawn into closer cooperation with the united Common Market through their own self-interest. There are already many signs that this is happening, such as a series of trade agreements in recent years between the Common Market countries and the Soviet bloc. In addition, the United States and Japan have shown renewed interest in helping

Russia to develop her natural resources, especially in Siberia. Brandt also sees the Soviet desire for a European security conference, recently begun at Helsinki, Finland, as a sign of Soviet willingness to come to a livable arrangement with the West.

Progress toward unity with the Soviet Union is slow, but Brandt thinks that it will be speeded up. He believes that as the Western European nations become more united they will draw Eastern Europe closer. As the Soviet bloc nations continue their internal transformation and become less dogmatic, contacts with the West will become easier. It is for these reasons that Brandt has insisted that West Germany pay the heavy price of recognizing that its lost territories are really lost and of reopening contacts with the Eastern nations.

Brandt is completely opposed to the old Cold War approach to East European countries; he does not believe in isolating them, hoping that they will slowly suffer internal convulsions and collapse. That approach has only made them more suspicious and has hardened their dogmatic views. In short, as Brandt has often said, "The Cold War is over, the era of the détente has begun."

Brandt also sees a clear role for America in his new Europe. His speeches are filled with remarks about the need for close cooperation with the United States. But unlike earlier years, Brandt now sees the relationship between the United States and Western Europe as maturing and changing. Western Europe has grown into an equal partner with the United States and it has to be treated as such.

Although the Western Europeans still depend on the American atomic weapon shield for their protection, they have passed the stage where the United States can or should dominate them. For example, the Common Market of nine states today has a combined population of 250 million, which is larger than the United States. It sells more goods in the world than the United States and has two thirds of its economic production. In terms of most international standards of comparison, whether it is the number of medals won at the Olympic games, number of Nobel prizes in science, or the number of automobiles per person, the Common Market is nearly equal or superior to the United States and far ahead of the Soviet Union. This means, as Brandt remarked in his American visit of June, 1971, the sooner Western Europe speaks with one voice, the sooner "it will then carry part of the responsibility in world affairs which in the long term will also mean a reduction of the burden shouldered by the United States."

Brandt is personally very fond of the United States. He has received many awards here, including several honorary doctorates from American universities, and he has been honored with a number of triumphal parades. It was in the United States, during the bleak days of the Berlin crisis, that Brandt first developed his international reputation. He has shown his fondness for America by his public actions; unlike a number of European politicians, Brandt has never engaged in cheap anti-Americanism to win support at home. He has often cautioned the Germans that much of what they dislike and label American is in fact the product of a modern industrial society. Then, too, at the height of the Vietnam crisis, Brandt quietly suffered sharp attacks from many quarters because of his unwillingness to speak out against the war. Brandt was opposed to American involvement in Vietnam, but as a loyal ally he expressed his disagreements privately to the United States government and not to the press.

The appreciation Brandt has had for American aid since World War II was clearly indicated in 1972 at the Harvard commencement. On that occasion, the twenty-fifth anniversary of the Marshall Plan, Brandt pledged $47 million for the formation of an independent, American-run foundation to promote a deeper understanding between the United States and Europe. The gift from West Germany, he said, was to show that "our gratitude, the gratitude of Europeans, has remained alive." Brandt acknowledged in his speech that the Marshall Plan, which pumped $13.6 billion into war-torn Europe was perhaps the most crucial factor in its economic recovery and helped save Europe from falling under the control of the Soviet Union. It also "roused Europe's stifled self-confidence" and inspired the "vision of a Europe united in lasting peace."

Willy Brandt's historical importance has already been ensured. This unusual man, who rose from obscurity to international fame, is now compared favorably with Konrad Adenauer as the most important German in recent times. His name will always be associated with the Cold War as the valiant mayor of Berlin and, he hopes, as the man who ended it by his détente policies.

Abroad, Brandt, the holder of the Nobel Peace Prize, is seen as a symbol of the new Germany and of how well democracy has taken root in that once turbulent country. He is also seen as the "strong man of Europe" by many writers and leaders. Just as General Charles de Gaulle cast a long shadow over events in Europe in the 1960's, many expect Brandt to do so in the 1970's.

A Man for All Europe

Brandt has a powerful image in German politics. Few politicians have commanded the respect and admiration that he now has. Germans of all political parties look up to him as a national leader in a class by himself. To members of his own Social Democratic Party he is the hinge without which the party might split into two or three opposing factions.

But to the average German citizen, Brandt represents both the old and the new Germany. His solid figure, his typical German face, and his manner reassure many that thrift, hard work, and reasonableness, those old German qualities, have been combined with the new German qualities of humanitarianism, compassion, and justice.

Brandt's firm commitment to lead his people into a united Europe abroad and into a social democracy at home made many of his conservative fellow-citizens uneasy. But then every step into the unknown is uneasy, and this son of the Lübeck wharves, has known that for many years.

In May, 1974, Brandt, under pressure, resigned his position as chancellor. One of his most trusted assistants had been unmasked as a Communist spy, and this, plus certain personal problems, led him to the conclusion that his effectiveness as head of state would be impaired.

Rather than have this happen, Willy Brandt chose again to take another step into the unknown.

Glossary

Bundesrat	Upper house of the West German parliament appointed by the states (*Länder*).
Bundestag	Lower house of the West German parliament elected by popular vote.
CDU/CSU	Christian Democratic Union and its sister party, the Christian Social Union.
Coalition Government	Union of two or more parties to gain a ruling majority in the parliament.
Common Market	European Customs Union established in 1957 among West Germany, France, Italy, Belgium, the Netherlands, and Luxembourg.
DDR or GDR	German Democratic Republic, Deutsche Demokratische Republik, or East Germany.
FDP	Free Democratic Party, a major party in the West German parliament.
Grand Coalition	Union of the CDU/CSU and the SPD from 1966 to 1969.
NATO	North Atlantic Treaty Organization, formed in 1949 to protect Western Europe.
Nazi	National Socialist German Workers Party, Hitler's political movement which reigned from 1933 to 1945.
NDP	National Democratic Party, small radical right-wing party in West Germany.

Glossary

Ostpolitik	Brandt's new approach to Eastern European affairs.
SAP	Socialist Workers Party, small splinter party of the SPD.
SDS	Socialist German Students' League, radical left-wing party.
SED	Socialist Unity Party, or the ruling Communist Party in East Germany.
SHB	Social Democratic University League, a small student group formed by the SPD.
SPD	Social Democratic Party, Brandt's political party.
Third Reich	Name given to the Hitler period in Germany from 1933 to 1945.
Warsaw Pact	Treaty organized by the Soviet Union to oppose NATO.
Weimar Republic	Germany's first attempt at a republican form of government from 1919 to 1933.

Index

Adenauer, Konrad, 86, 90, 103, 152
  Brandt and, 89, 101, 104, 164
  chancellor, 77, 91, 100, 157
  Erhard and, 111, 115
Administrative Council, West Zone, 78
Adriatic Coast, Yugoslavia, 156
Africa, 129, 158
Allied Control Council, 59, 67, 74
Allies. *See* Western allies
Alsace-Lorraine, France, 19, 28
Ambassadors to Germany, 144
America, 17, 39, 75, 105, 157
  Kennedy and, 87, 89, 103, 107
  role in Europe, 162–164
  Schumacher and, 65–66.
  See also United States
American Freedom House Award, 91
Andernach, Germany, 24
Arbeiterbladet (newspaper), 37
Asia, 129, 158
Austria, 49, 56

Bach, Johann Sebastian, 144
Bad Godesberg, Germany, 86–87, 118, 140
Bad Kreuth, Germany, 142
Bahr, Egon, 125
Baltic Sea, 24, 36
Baltimore Sun, 138
Barcelona, Spain, 47
Barlach, Ernst, 43
Barzel, Rainer, 134–137
Basic Law (*Grundgesetz*), 78–79
Basic Treaty, 134–136
Bebel, August, 18
Beethoven, Ludwig van, 70, 144
Belgium, 157
Berlin, Germany
  access agreement, 127, 129–130
  airlift, 75–76
  blockade, 74–76, 94, 97
  Brandt in, 57, 62, 79, 91, 145–146, 149, 152–153
  crisis, 98–102, 105, 163
  cultural life, 42–44
  description of (modern), 61, 64, 92–110
  description of (1940's), 66–70
  description of (1930's), 33–35, 44–46
  Federal Law, 80
  history of, 20–21
  organization, 59, 77, 81
  people, 83–85
  problem, 89, 101, 129
  transit agreement, 132.
  See also East Berlin, West Berlin, Lord mayor of Berlin
Berlin-Capital City competition, 93
Berlin Christian Democratic Party, 101
Berlin City Assembly, 79
Berlin City Hall, 108–109
Berlin House of Representatives, 79–80, 83
Berlin Municipal Assembly, 77
Berlin Parliament, 79
Berlin Philharmonic, 143–144
Berlin Senate, 93
Berlin Wall, 91, 95, 104–108, 125–126, 145
Bernstein, Eduard, 15
Big Four Occupying Powers, 127
Bismarck, Otto von, 90
Blubo literature, 43
Blunck, Hans Friedrich, 43
Böll, Heinrich, 70
Bonhoeffer, Dietrich, 43
Bonn, Germany, 79–80, 86, 94, 98, 113, 146
Brandenburg Gate, 84
Brecht, Bertolt, 21
Bremen, Germany, 62
Brezhnev, Leonid, 130

168

Index

Buchenwald Concentration Camp, 44
Bundesrat, 79–80
Bundestag, 79–83, 86, 122–123, 131–135, 149.
See also Elections
CDU/CSU. See Christian Democratic Party
Chancellor Brandt, 122–165.
See also Elections
Checkpoint Charlie, 105, 108.
See also Berlin, West Berlin
Christ und Welt, 154
Christian Democratic Party (CDU/CSU), 86, 90, 115–116, 121, 133–135, 137–138.
See also Coalition government, Elections, Grand coalition
Citizenship of Brandt, 54–55, 71, 90
Clay, Lucius D., 63
Coalition government, 115–119, 121–122, 133, 136.
See also CDU/CSU, Grand coalition, Elections
Cold War, 65, 69, 74, 117, 129
Berlin and, 92–97
Brandt and, 101, 124, 136, 138, 162, 164
Cologne, Germany, 61, 92
Common Market, 87, 97, 115, 122, 157–163
Community of the Ten, 158
Communist Party of Germany (DKP), 35, 65, 130, 138
Communists, 48, 77, 84, 88, 104, 106, 108, 128
Constitution for West Germany, 71, 77–78
Cooper, James Fenimore, 22
Copenhagen, Denmark, 40–41, 62.
See also Denmark
Costa Brava, Spain, 156
Council of Europe, 124
Council for Mutual Economic Assistance, 97
Council of States, 78
Cuba, 107
Cultural exchanges, 159–160
Czechoslovakia, 39, 49, 56, 118, 124–125

Day of German Unity, 82
de Gaulle, Charles, 103, 115, 124, 154, 156, 164

Denmark, 19, 35–36, 56–57, 64, 143, 158.
See also Copenhagen, Denmark, Scandinavia
Der Spiegel affair, 111
Deutschland, Deutschland über Alles, 70
Domestic policy of Germany
  Der Spiegel, 111
  economic reform, 87
  education, 100, 118, 139
  social reform, 61, 87, 122–123, 137, 141
  United States, 164
Dortmund, Germany, 114
Dovre Prisoner of War Camp, 53
Dresden, Germany, 33–34
Dulles, John Foster, 89

Early life of Brandt, 13–35, 41, 149.
See also Personal life of Brandt
East Berlin, Germany, 74, 81, 94–95, 98, 126.
See also Berlin, East Germany
East Germans, 117–118, 120, 132, 145
East Germany
  Berlin and, 74–76, 92, 94–99, 103–106
  frontiers of, 59
  Ostpolitik and, 124–126
  People's Police, 84, 96, 104–105
  postwar problems, 96–98
  SPD, 65
  treaties, 127–130, 135
  unification, 80–84.
See also East Berlin, Germany
East-West German relations, 102, 107, 117–118, 124–136, 159
Eastern European nations, 61, 94, 117–118, 123–129, 154–162
Ebert, Friedrich, 19, 119
Economic Council, 78
Education of Brandt, 13, 21–23, 26, 28, 31, 41, 48.
See also Johanneum
Education in Germany, 118, 139–140
Einstein, Albert, 42
Eisenhower, Dwight D., 89
Eiserne Front, 30
Elections
  in 1961, 88–91, 104, 153

in 1965, 111–116, 153
in 1969, 119–121
in 1972, 136–138
Elster, Torolf, 55
Enderle, August, 35
England, 39, 52, 59, 66, 75, 122, 129, 158
English, 17, 65–66
Erfurt, Germany, 125–126
Erhard, Ludwig, 111–112, 115–116
Erler, Fritz, 88
Europe, 13, 39, 64, 74, 107, 131, 157
  unity of, 58, 96, 118, 124, 156, 158–165
European Economic Community.
  See Common Market
Exile of Brandt, 36–46

Family of Brandt
  Carlota (wife), 50–51, 53, 55–57
  father, 16, 19
  grandfather, 14–19, 21, 23, 41
  half-brother, 21, 62
  Lars (son), 112–113, 146–148
  Matthias (son), 146, 148
  mother, 16, 21, 26, 41, 58, 62, 71
  Ninja (daughter), 57
  Peter (son), 76, 146–149
  Rut (wife), 73, 75–76, 85, 88, 99, 142, 145–157, 151, 156
  stepgrandmother, 19
  stepfather, 21, 41, 62
Family life, 37, 56–57, 90, 142, 145–149
Fascists, 47–49
Federal Republic of Germany. *See* West Berlin, West Germany
Finland, 55.
  See also Scandinavia
Foreign minister, 101, 119–120, 122, 132
  Brandt as, 117, 124, 146–147, 158.
  See also Ministers
Foreign policy of Germany, 74–76, 86–89, 101–138, 156–164
Four-Power Pact, 130
Four Powers in Berlin, 99, 130, 132
France, 19, 39, 48–49, 56, 65–66, 115, 124, 157
Franco-German relations, 132, 159–160
Frankfurt, Germany, 107
Free Democratic Party (FDP), 115–116, 119, 121, 136, 138.
  See also SPD/FDP

Free Trade Union Federation, 32, 81
Free University of West Berlin, 109, 148, 150
Free World, 108
Freiburg, Germany, 29
French Alps, 156
French foreign minister, 157
French occupation, 20
Friends of Brandt
  Gertrude, 37, 41
  Nazi period, 33–36, 40
  Norway, 39, 44–46, 51–53
  politics, 62, 66–69, 124, 137, 143–144, 151, 153
  Scandinavia, 31, 132
  Sweden, 54–55
  youth, 28–30
Froehlich, Paul, 35

Geneva, Switzerland, 101–102
George, Stefan, 46
German armed forces, 29, 50–51, 57, 111
German Democratic Republic.
  See Germany, East Germany
German Federal Republic.
  See Germany, West Germany
German-French exchanges, 159–160
German High Court, 78
German News Agency, 144
German-Soviet relations, 127, 130, 133
Germany
  Brandt and, 62–63, 71–72, 143, 154–155
  citizenship, 136
  currency, 74, 123
  economic growth, 21, 94–95
  history, 92–93
  inflation, 21, 137
  national anthem, 70, 85
  Nazism in, 27, 31–32, 34–35, 37, 39, 42–45, 49
  postwar problems, 19, 60–61, 67, 69–70, 73, 77
  recession, 115–117
  reconstruction of, 55–72
  reunification of, 59, 80–82, 87, 96–98, 102, 117, 126, 132, 135–136
  states, 77, 79.
  See also East Germany, Nazis, West Germany

Index

Goals for Europe, 67, 156–158, 161–162
Goering, Hermann, 63
Goethe, Johann Wolfgang von, 19, 28
Gottgetreu, Jacob, 22
Grand coalition, 116–119.
  See also Christian Democratic Party, Coalition government, Elections
Grass, Günter, 70, 117, 137, 143, 147
Grieg, Edvard, 144
Grotewohl, Otto, 65
Group '47, 69
Guadalajara, Spain, 47
Guttmann, Simon, 20

Hague, The, Netherlands, 158
Hamburg, Germany, 43, 61, 92
Hansa Quarter, Berlin, 93
Harpprecht, Klaus, 23
Hauptmann, Gerhart, 43
Heinemann, Gustav, 119
Helsinki, Finland, 162.
  See also Finland, Scandinavia
Hesse, Germany, 116
Heuss, Theodor, 70, 77
Hitler, Adolf
  Brandt and, 52, 154
  chancellor, 32, 40
  Mein Kampf, 45
  Mussolini and, 49
  Nobel Prize, 42
  Third Reich of, 33, 37, 39, 44, 70, 72, 85
  World War II, 51, 55–57, 69
  youth groups and, 27
Hochhuth, Rolf, 112
Holland, 39
Home of Brandt, 14–16, 21, 37, 45, 50, 53, 55, 73, 75–76, 145–147
Hundred Days, 123
Hungarian uprisings, 84, 96
Hungary, 56, 84

Iceland, 56
Image of Brandt, 87–88, 123
Interests of Brandt, 22–23, 142–155
  hobbies, 143
  music, 143–144
  reading, 22, 24, 45, 143, 145.
  See also Personal life of Brandt
International Circle of Democratic Socialists, 56

International reputation of Brandt, 128–129, 131–133, 136, 138, 153–165.
  See also Press
International Workers' Council, 57
Ireland, 158
Iron Curtain, 94–95, 104
Italy, 157

Japan, 161
Jews, 34, 127
Johanneum, 22–23, 26, 28, 48.
  See also Education of Brandt
Johnson, Lyndon, 105–106, 109, 115

Kassel, Germany, 125–126
Keitel, Wilhelm, 63
Kennedy, Jacqueline, 109–110
Kennedy, John F., 87, 89, 91, 102–110, 112, 154
Kennedy, Robert, 106, 110
Khrushchev, Nikita, 98–103, 106, 153
Kiesinger, Kurt Georg, 116–117
Kirchner, Ernst Ludwig, 43
Kolbe, Georg, 43
Kollwitz, Käthe, 43
Kosygin, Aleksei, 127

Lage, 144
Landsberg Prison, 45
Lange, Halvard, 39, 66, 70–71
Langhelle, Nils, 39
Languages of Brandt, 39, 45, 100, 117, 150, 155–156
Lasalle, Ferdinand, 18
Latin America, 158
Leber, Julius, 22, 28–33, 38
Leipzig, Germany, 43
Lie, Trygve, 52, 55
Lillehammer, Norway, 52
London, England, 51, 55, 92, 130
London Daily Mirror, 138
London Guardian, 123
Lord mayor of Berlin
  Brandt as, 83–85, 92–117, 126, 148, 151–152, 164
  Reuter as, 68, 77
  Suhr as, 83, 86
Lübeck, Germany, 13–35, 41, 62, 66, 165
Lübeck Social Democrats, 28.
  See also Social Democratic Party
Lübeck Socialist Worker Party, 34

Luxembourg, 157

Macmillan, Harold, 101, 103
Mann, Golo, 117
Mann, Heinrich, 44
Mann, Thomas, 22, 42, 44, 117
Marshall, George, 74
Marshall Plan, 94, 157, 164
Marxism, 18, 36, 87, 140
Meckel, Christoph, 93
Mecklenburg, Germany, 16, 21
Medborgarhuset, Stockholm, Sweden, 56
Middle East, 129
Middle Germany, 124
Military Mission, Allied Control Council, 67, 73-74
Ministerial Council of East Germany, 125
Ministry of All-German Affairs, 124
Ministry of Inter-German Relations, 124
Monnet, Jean, 157
Moe, Finn, 37-38
Moscow, Russia, 48, 101, 125-127, 129, 133-136.
See also Russia, Soviet Union
Mot Dag, 40
Munich, Germany, 21, 92, 136
Mussolini, Benito, 49
Myrdal, Alva, 132
Myrdal, Gunnar, 55, 132

Nachrichtenspiegel, 144
Name of Brandt, 13, 19, 26, 33-34, 37, 44, 71, 90
National Democratic Party (NPD), 115, 138
Nazi People's Court, 33
Nazis
 arts of, 60, 70
 attitudes toward, 45, 116-117
 Berlin, 34, 123, 155
 black list, 37
 concentration camps, 65, 131
 flight from, 51-54
 growth of, 26-27, 36, 72
 Nuremberg War Trials, 63-65
 prisons, 88
 SAP bases, 35, 37
 strength of, 30-33
 storm troopers, 32
 violence of, 40, 42

World War II, 49-57.
See also Germany
Nerman, Ture, 54
Netherlands, 157
New York, 120
Newsweek (magazine), 123
Nexo, Andersen, 22
Nobel Foundation, 50
Nobel Peace Prize, 42-43, 131-132, 163-164
Non-Proliferation of Atomic Weapons Treaty, 159
Nordens Frihet (magazine), 54
North Atlantic Treaty Organization (NATO), 87, 97, 118
North Rhine-Westphalia, Germany, 115
North Sea, 24, 51
Norway
 Brandt in, 37-44, 49-53, 58, 62, 73, 85, 121, 145, 156
 citizenship, 52, 70, 131
 Common Market, 158, 161
 government of, 42, 54, 66, 131
 king of, 51-52
 Nobel Peace Prize, 42
 SAP bases, 37-38
 SPD, 64-65
 World War II, 49-58, 132
 youth movements, 38-39, 73.
 See also Oslo, Norway, Scandinavia
Norwegian Embassy, 51, 66, 73
Norwegian Public Relief, 39
Norwegian resistance movement, 54
Norwegian Social Democratic Party Press, 63
Norwegian Spanish Committee, 49
Norwegian Workers' Party, 39
Norwegian Youth Federation, 39
Norwegians, 40, 55, 69, 144
Nuclear weapons ban, 87
Nuremberg War Trials, 63-66

Occupation powers, 65
Official Policy Statement, 138-139
Ollenhauer, Erich, 65, 88, 111
Olympic Games, 44, 136, 163
Operation Vittles, 75
Organization Metro, 44
Oslo, Norway
 Brandt in, 37-44, 49-51, 53, 58, 62, 73
 intellectual life, 40

Index

Nobel Peace Prize, 131–132
SAP bases, 35, 37–38, 41
Spanish Civil War, 47
World War II, 49–58.
See also Norway, Scandinavia
Ossietzky, Carl von, 42, 131–132
Ostpolitik (Eastern Policy), 117, 124, 128–129, 133–136, 159

Palais Schaumburg, 144, 146
Palestine, 56
Paris, France, 21, 66, 92, 102, 130
Parliamentary Council, 78–79
Paul, Ernst, 54
People's Aid, 52
People's Revolt, East Germany, 81–83
Permanent Economic Commission, 78
Personal life of Brandt, 142–156.
See also Early life of Brandt, Interests of Brandt
Personality of Brandt, 22–23, 119–121, 150–155, 165
Planck, Max, 43
Poland, 19, 50, 124, 127, 133
Polish-West German Treaty, 127–130
Potsdam Conference, 59, 98
President of Germany, 77, 89, 119
Press, 66, 113–114, 123, 136–138, 147, 149, 159, 164.
See also International reputation
Preuss, Hugo, 20
Propaganda for the West, 95
Prussia, 92
Prussian State Library, 45

Quidde, Ludwig, 132

Rathenau, Walter, 20–21
Red Falcons, 24
Refugee organizations, 38, 54
Refugees, 64, 77, 95–96, 104–105, 131, 133
Reichsbanner, 30
Reichsgründungsfeier, 26
Reichstag, 27–28, 32, 65
Reinhardt, Max, 43
Remarque, Erich Maria, 22, 154
Reuter, Ernst, 68–69, 75–77, 83
Rhine River, 24
Rhineland, 49
Ribbentrop, Joachim von, 63
Richter, Hans Werner, 112
Rilke, Rainer Maria, 24
River Spree, 105
Rome-Berlin Axis, 49
Ruhr, 20
Rumania, 118
Russia, 13, 59, 88, 157, 161–162
  Berlin and, 67, 74–75, 102, 105–107, 129, 133
  Brandt and, 80
  East Germany, 81
  German unity, 82–83
  Hungarian uprising, 84–85
  territories, 127, 133.
  See also Moscow, Russia, Soviet Union
Russian zone, 66

St. Paul's Cathedral, Frankfurt, 107
Sauckel, Fritz, 63
Scandinavia, 13, 19, 31, 39, 50, 67, 75, 121, 132, 143, 146.
  See also Denmark, Finland, Norway, Sweden
Scandinavian newspapers, 47, 65–66
Scheel, Walter, 122, 127
Schiller, Friedrich von, 19
Schiller, Karl, 88, 122–123, 136
Schleswig, Germany, 19
Schmidt, Helmut, 88, 122
Schoneberg, Berlin, Germany, 84
Schumacher, Kurt, 65–66
Schuman, Robert, 157
Second German Empire, 26
Sewerun, Rakel, 39
Siberia, 162
Smear campaigns, 90, 114, 152
Social Democrat, 79
Social Democratic *Kinderfreunde*, 24
Social Democratic Parliamentary Group, 83
Social Democratic Party (SPD)
  Berlin and, 101
  Brandt in, 13, 65, 70, 79, 87–88, 101, 111, 121, 165
  building party, 64–65, 72, 87–89, 114–115, 122
  coalition government and, 116–119, 121
  elections and, 86, 88–90, 107, 111–113
  history of, 17–18

membership, 28, 140
Nazis and, 27–28, 30–31
philosophy of, 68, 86–88
Scandinavia, 54–56, 65
Socialist Workers Party, 30, 35, 37
youth organizations, 23–27, 30, 150
Social Democratic University League (SHB), 118
Social Democrats–Free Democrats SPD/FDP), 121–122, 133
Socialist Committee in Paris, 42
Socialist German Students' League (SDS), 118
Socialist Unity Party (SED), 65
Socialist Workers Party (SAP), 30–31, 33, 35, 37, 47, 151
Soviet treaty, 127–130
Soviet Union
  Berlin and, 66–67, 94–106
  Brandt and, 123–124, 152–153, 156
  Cold War, 74, 117
  Czechoslovakia, 118
  leaders of, 97–99
  united Europe, 161, 164.
  See also Moscow, Russia
Spain, 47, 49, 56
Spanish Civil War, 47–49
SPD. *See* Social Democratic Party, Elections
Splinter party groups, 118–119
Stahlhelm, 30
Stalin, Joseph, 48, 84
State of the Nation Address, 128
Stevenson, Adlai, 114
Stockholm, Sweden, 50, 53–58, 73, 131.
  See also Scandinavia, Sweden
Stoph, Willi, 125
Strasbourg, France, 29
Strauss, Richard, 43
Stresemann, Gustav, 132
Strobel, Käte, 122
Student riots, 118–119
Stuttgart, Germany, 61, 154
Sudetenland, 56
Suhr, Otto, 83, 86
Summit Conference, Paris, 102
Sweden, 51–58, 64–65, 73, 88, 131, 156.
  See also Scandinavia, Stockholm, Sweden
Swedish government, 42
Swedish-Norwegian Press Agency, 54
Switzerland, 49

Test Ban Treaty, 107
Third Reich, 33, 40, 44, 64
Third World, 118
Time (magazine), Man of the Year, 128
Treaty of Versailles, 19
Trondheim, Norway, 57
Tucholsky, Kurt, 43
Turkey, 68

Ulbricht, Walter, 105, 129
Union of Ships' Pilots, 154
United Marxist Labor Party, 48
United Nations, 55, 63, 84, 100, 106, 135
United Nations General Assembly, 120
United States, 59, 129, 147, 161
  Brandt in, 55, 99–100, 145
  Common Market, 115, 158
  Harvard Commencement, 164
  World War II, 52, 56, 74.
  See also America
United States of Europe, 157
United States–German relations, 103, 118
United States–Russian relations, 103, 105–107
University of Freiburg, Germany, 29
University of Oslo, Norway, 41
University of Strasbourg, France, 29
Urals, 156

Vice chancellor, 117, 122
Vienna, Austria, 103
Vietnam, 147, 163–164
Volksbote (SPD paper), 22, 28–30
Volkswagen, 154
Voting age, 120

Walcher, Jacob, 35
Warsaw, Poland, 127
Warsaw Pact, 97, 117
Warsaw treaties, 133–136
Washington, D. C., 130
Washington News, 154
Wehner, Herbert, 88
Weimar Republic, 19–23, 26, 72, 112, 117, 149
Weiss, Peter, 112
Weltbühne (newspaper), 42
West Berlin, 80, 92, 110, 130.
  See also Berlin, West Germany
West Berlin police, 105

Index

West German government, 78–79, 86, 121–122, 128, 131
West German Parliament, 127
West German–Soviet treaty, 127
West Germany
  Berlin and, 98–99
  East German relations with, 127–130, 135, 145
  founding, 89, 138
  refugees in, 95, 104
  writers of, 23, 112, 137, 153.
    See also Domestic policy, Foreign policy, Germany, West Berlin
West Zone, 78, 81
Western allies
  Basic Treaty, 135
  Berlin, 74–76, 97–99, 101–102, 105–107
  Brandt and, 67, 70
  Russia, 69, 74, 82, 124, 129, 131, 133, 161
  World War I, 19
  World War II, 60, 77–78
Western European nations, 158, 162
Wiechert, Ernst, 43
Wilhelm II, Kaiser, 15
Workers' Mandolin Club, 24
Workers' Sport Association, 23

World War I, 15, 19, 21
World War II, 47–58, 60, 72, 96, 156–157, 164
  defeat of Germany, 128, 132–133.
    See also Refugees
Writings of Brandt, 54, 61–62, 67, 72
  books
    After Germany, 58
    Criminals and the "Other" Germans, The, 66
    From Bonn to Berlin, 80–81
    Guerillakriget, 85
    In Exile, 71
    War Aims of the Great Powers and the New Europe, 51
  newspaper articles, 22, 28, 38, 40, 53–54
  Nuremberg War Trials reporting, 63–64
  pamphlets, 40, 48–50, 55–56
  Social Democrat, 79
  Swedish-Norwegian Press Agency, 54

Youth and Brandt, 47–48, 64, 120, 148–150
Yugoslavia, 118, 156